Wisdom and politics of a practical person
Sermons of Pamela Fulton

Wisdom and politics of a practical person
Sermons of Pamela Fulton

Pamela Fulton

Copyright © 2012, Anna Messner

All rights reserved. No part of this book may be reproduced, stored, or transmitted by any means—whether auditory, graphic, mechanical, or electronic—without written permission of both publisher and author, except in the case of brief excerpts used in critical articles and reviews. Unauthorized reproduction of any part of this work is illegal and is punishable by law.

ISBN 978-1-105-47298-5

*In memory of Pamela Fulton (1939 – 2009)
wife, mother, friend, and minister*

Introduction

Pam Fulton was born on April 14, 1939. She grew up mostly in New York with her parents Ruth and Robert (Bob) Fulton and her younger brother William (Bill) Fulton. Her father was a businessman and her mother a homemaker. Her family moved to Mexico just before her senior year of high school so she went to a boarding school for that year. As a teenager Pam was interested in becoming a Christian minister but was strongly discouraged from pursuing this career path because the ministry was not considered an option for women at the time. She matriculated at Skidmore College in Saratoga Springs, New York where she met A. Arendt Hopeman, III who was attending nearby Hamilton College. As many young women did at the time, she dropped out of college after her sophomore year to marry Arendt. Nine months and 2 days later she gave birth to the first of five children she had with him. The children were born every 2 years beginning in 1960 and are named Anna, Susan, Albert Arendt IV (A.A.), Leslie and Robert (Bob). Having 5 children over 8 years kept Pam busy. One winter, when there were 4 children, each child came down with mumps, then chicken pox, Sue had pneumonia, A.A. pulled his arm out of its socket, and Pam had a miscarriage. Pam said she was ready to quit motherhood at that point—fortunately she did not. When Bob started kindergarten Pam went back to school at the University of Rochester. An amazing organizer, she spent her days caring for children (driving them to the seemingly endless activities,) going to school, and taking care of the house. Usually a fabulous cook, these were the crock-pot years (not the highlight of her culinary career). She graduated with a degree in Political Science and went on to get a master's degree in Public Policy Studies. Pam was also active in local political organizations in Rochester, NY where the family lived. In 1981 the family moved to Waynesboro, Virginia for Arendt's work. The couple separated and then divorced a year later after 23 years of marriage.

After a time of reflection, Pam returned to Rochester where she enrolled in the Colgate Rochester Divinity School. Upon graduation, she moved to Lansing, Michigan to take a position at Westminster Presbyterian Church as an assistant pastor. With the backing of the church and its congregation, Pam founded several programs dedicated to helping the people of the community. Advent House Ministries runs a weekend day shelter for people in need, a clothes closet, provides temporary housing for homeless people as well as work programs for people who have none. Pam was passionate in her drive to counteract the injustice she saw in the world and improve the lives of those who have less. While in Lansing, she met Ed Havitz, a retired middle school teacher, and they married in 1989.

Pam and Ed were active in their care of the people who came to Advent House, including 2 children, Faith and Jimmy Morgan. The Morgan children's mother had difficulty caring for them at that time and eventually Pam and Ed legally adopted Jimmy and Faith when they were 12 and 9 years of age. After several years in Lansing, Pam and Ed decided to move the family to Manistique in the Upper Peninsula of Michigan where Pam became the minister of Presbyterian Church of the Redeemer. They raised Jimmy and Faith and again Pam and Ed were active in local charitable organizations—particularly Habitat for Humanity. Ed, during this time, was in the relatively early stages of Alzheimer's disease which began to progress. After Jimmy and Faith graduated from high school and moved on, Pam retired from the ministry—temporarily. After approximately 2 years of retirement she and Ed (who was declining due to the Alzheimer's) moved to Lake Leelanau, MI where they lived across the street from Ed's daughter Lynn Hansen. Pam began working again helping out churches that were temporarily without a minister. In April 2009, Pam became ill, was diagnosed with metastatic malignant melanoma, and passed away 1 month later on May 7, 2009. At the time her terminal diagnosis was made Pam was active in her community and church and was even scheduled to start teaching a water aerobics class the following month. Though she struggled with the knowledge that she was going to die she said that her last ministry was to show people how to die with dignity—which she did. In the process of cleaning out her house her children came across a filing cabinet filled with old sermons. We have chosen our favorites for this book.

Anna Hopeman Messner

January, 2012

Lessons

1. Blessed to receive
- help we get, angels don't take $. God's gift of Christ
2. We don't have to decide
want our Bible heroes to be GOOD
"how faith moves in the seasons of experience" Brueggemann
deserving? It's not up to us to decide if people deserve our love - that's up to God!
3. Reflections - God present in the mountains - at bottom of any decision fatigue down to ministry

1. 1
2. 5
3. 9
4. Beware 13
5. Journey in the spirit 17
6. A Sanctuary for childhood 21
7. Homosexuality, the Bible, and the Church 25
8. The Food at your door (Thanksgiving) 29
9. Crying in the wilderness 31
10. A Messy affair 35
11. To Grieve our saints 39
12. An Invitation 45
13. The Gospel is political 49
14. Those people 53
15. Called by name 57
16. Final words 63

It is also blessed to receive

Isaiah 9:2-7, Luke 2:1-20

December 24, 1987

The time has come, the waiting ends. Tonight is the night of wonder, of splendor, of deep peace. Preparations have ceased— or at least been abandoned, and it's time to settle into the mystery, to follow the start to Bethlehem, and to join the crowd gathering around the manger.

Tonight is a night for gifts; gifts to be given and gifts received. Children can't sleep for wondering what they will get. Parents eagerly anticipate their children's reactions to the gifts they've chosen. It's a mark of maturity I guess, to anticipate the joy that comes in giving gifts more than the joy that comes from getting gifts.

It *is* more blessed to give than to receive. But in our excitement and anticipation over giving we sometimes lose sight of the fact that it is also blessed to receive. Sometimes we don't know how to receive gifts.

I imagine most of you have had the experience of giving someone a gift and having them say, "Oh, you shouldn't have" or "Oh, you shouldn't have spent so much money on me." Deflating responses aren't they? They take the wind right out of your sails and the joy out of your giving. How about responses such as "Oh, I don't deserve such a nice gift" or "This gift is much too good for me to use, I'm going to save it for a special occasion." And you know that person will go to his or her grave never having used your gift.

There are different kinds of responses – ones that let you know immediately that you've goofed. They go something like "What is it?" or "Why did you get me this?" Then there are those, usually children but not always, who misuse your gift and immediately break it.

Trying to give others the gift of help can be even worse. Some people assume that to accept help from another implies weakness on their part, and their pride is hurt if you offer to help them. Others assume that a gift—whether it be one that comes in a package, or an offer of help—must be paid back in kind, that to accept the gift obligates one in some way.

When we respond in ways like these, we forget that in receiving gifts ungraciously because of our own embarrassment and awkwardness or our sense of unworthiness we rob the giver of the joy of giving. To receive a gift graciously, is to give a gift—the gift of delight, of welcome, of warmth, of admiration and respect and love for the giver.

Let me tell you about a lady who knew how to receive gifts. When my children were young, we lived right around the corner from their great-grandmother and one of them had dinner with her nearly every night of the week. NayNay, as we called her, was a great lady, a woman of great charm and a lover of beauty. She was a woman of wealth with exquisite taste and much fine jewelry.

When my youngest son, Bob, was six or seven, his school had a "Secret Santa Sale," a place where children could buy gifts to fit their budgets. Bob came home from school one day in a state of great excitement and euphoria. He had bought NayNay a huge "diamond" ring for ten cents. The chrome paint was already peeling off the sides.

On Christmas Eve Bob gave NayNay her diamond ring with bated breath and all the pride and love a seven-year-old could muster. And for months afterward, every time Bob went to see NayNay she replaced her lovely expensive ring with the ten-cent diamond. When she died several years later, the ten-cent diamond lay at the top of her jewelry box. And Bob knew that he had given a good gift, that he had pleased the one he loved, and that she loved him.

Tonight is a night for gifts, gifts to be given and gifts received. Tonight God gives us a gift—a gift of a child, a tiny baby who is the very self of God. Tonight God gives us the gift of one who will love us as we've never been loved before, who will die for us, who will rise for us, who will reign in power for us, who will pray for us.

How will we receive this gift that God wants to give us? Will we say, "Oh no God, you shouldn't have?" Will we refuse to accept the gift because we think ourselves unworthy? Will we refuse to accept the gift for fear of the kind of obligations we think might be tied to it? Will we deprive God of the joy of giving freely to us? Or will we take that tiny baby of God into our arms, feel the warmth and life of him, smell the smell of Mary's milk on him, examine his fingernails and count his toes and say to God, "Thank you God, this baby is what I wanted most in the world and I will love him with my whole heart forever."

Tonight is a night for gifts; gifts to be given and gifts received. This night, let us receive our gifts with wonder and love and graciousness, and all the thanks we are capable of giving.

Thanks be to God.

Pam, NayNay, and baby Anna 1960

Something we don't have to decide

Genesis 27:1-27a, Luke 18:9-14, Psalm 146

June 28, 1987

The story of Jacob and Esau is not a lectionary passage. For those of you who do not know what the lectionary is, it's a three-year cycle of Bible readings for each Sunday and special worship day. The intent of the lectionary is to have read in the worship of the church over a three-year period the great biblical texts affirming the central themes of the Christian faith. There are some advantages to using the lectionary. For one, a congregation will probably be exposed to a greater breadth of passages than if the preacher just picks her or his own favorites and, secondly, it forces the preacher to deal with subjects and passages he or she might prefer to avoid

Around here, Phil Henderson and I use the lectionary much of the time but we don't feel tied to it because it has disadvantages too. The most important of which is that great chunks of the bible never get read—like the story of Jacob and Esau. I guess it would be hard to slot that story of conniving and duplicity into one of the great themes of Christian faith.

The lectionary also doesn't include the story of Jacob's use of creative sheep breeding to enlarge his own flocks at the expense of his father-in-law, Laban. That story is told in Chapter 31 of Genesis and I'll let you read it rather than taking the time to tell it to you now.

The lectionary tends to "accentuate the positive." The Jacob stories which it does include are Jacob's ladder and Jacob wrestling with God at Peniel. If those were the only stories we knew of Jacob we would be tempted to think he was a very good and godly man. That's a real human tendency, isn't it. To want our Bible heroes, or our heroes of any kind, to be all good. Jacob was one of the patriarchs of our faith, the son of Isaac, the grandson of Abraham, the father of the twelve tribes of Israel. Would God have used someone who was as dishonest and scheming and self-interested as Jacob to father the nation of Israel? Hard to accept, isn't it? How do we draw morals from this lesson? It doesn't even do us much good to compare ourselves to Jacob because he got the rewards, and what do we get for being good?

Walter Brueggemann, in his commentary on Genesis, has this to say about this story: "…the narrator does not explain or justify. Indeed, the narrator seems unaware of the incongruity that may appear to us: a blessing gotten by deception! While that may be a problem for us, we do better to stay inside the story itself, to perceive that the narrative is simply that way (as is life itself)… (Genesis) is not a spiritual treatise on morality. It is, rather, a memory of how faith moves in the rawness of experience. We must leave it at that."

Maybe that's why Genesis is one of my favorite books of the Bible—because its characters are so human. They're a mixture of good and bad as we all are. Its characters struggle with God, and turn away from God, and come back to God, as most of us do. They're not the simple, one-dimensional storybook people we sometimes think they should be.

In our terms we'd probably say Jacob and perhaps the other patriarchs as well didn't deserve to be God's chosen people. But whether they deserve it or not is not for us to decide. That's for God to decide.

So it is today. We often want people to be good or bad, deserving or undeserving. We want to know if people deserve what they're getting. This becomes especially important when we're giving of ourselves. We want to know if the people we help "deserve it." There's a local foundation in Lansing which gives its money to organizations serving "worthy, indigent, older people." I wonder how they decide who is worthy and who is not.

The thing that always intrigues me is the fact that it's easier to decide who's deserving with less information. If all we knew of Jacob was the lectionary passages we'd decide he's deserving; if all we knew were the Esau and Laban passages we'd decide he's undeserving. When we know the whole story Jacob becomes a complex person about whom it becomes exceedingly difficult to make judgments.

Let me give you a modern example. Robert Trevino is a 39-year-old Hispanic male who was a frequent guest at Advent House. On May 2 he broke into our church and stole two bags of food. At first, we thought he must have been hungry and maybe had a hungry family to provide for. We later learned that he has no family and indeed he had picked up a food order at the food bank at Cristo Rey that very day. We also learned that he was drunk when he did it and that he's an ex-convict. In fact he's been in prison more than he's been out. We also learned rather quickly that he's an alcoholic, that he's made no attempt to find work since getting out of prison the last time, and that he's the father of a one-year-old girl whose mother will not let Robert near her. He's now in Ingham County jail awaiting trial. Not a very good person is he? Not a very deserving person.

Now let's try this story with more information. And I do want you to know that I have Bobby's permission to tell you his story. Bobby Trevino was born in Mississippi in 1958 and his mother died when he was an infant. His father remarried and brought Bobby and his older brother and stepmother to Jackson, Michigan where Bobby grew up. When he and his brother were children they often had to steal food because their parents wouldn't give them enough to eat. Bobby has scars on his body where he was beaten both at home and in school. He spent eleven years in special education classes where he was labeled a slow learner and where his teachers told him "You'll never be able to learn anything." He used to climb out the windows of his classroom and crawl along the wall of the school building just before school was out so the other kids wouldn't see him coming out and beat him up or tease him about being in special ed classes.

Bobby learned very early that he couldn't trust people and he became very much a loner. That was obvious when he came to Advent House. He was always pleasant, polite, and occasionally offered to help but he always came and left by himself and was very quiet. He says now with surprising perceptiveness that he always gets in trouble when his relationships with others are in trouble. He spent quite some time bumming around the country on his own and had no difficulty staying out of trouble then.

Bobby also learned to cope with his problems by drinking. He drank heavily even as a child. He's made attempts at not drinking, gone to lots of AA meetings, but has never been able to stay dry for very long. He talks with surprising eloquence about how being in prison and being an alcoholic are alike. "In both cases," he says, "you're in darkness. You cannot see the beauty of nature or the beauty in other people."

Bobby was in a severe car accident as a teenager and has pins in both arms and his leg which kept him from joining the army, something he very much wanted to do.

Bobby got in trouble early on and landed in Jackson prison when he was 18 years old—not a good place in which to grow up. He's spent a lot of years in prison and acknowledges that he's often more comfortable there. It's not that he actually likes it, but he does know where his next meal is coming from and what he's expected to do. It's secure. He doesn't have to make decisions and he doesn't have to deal with those difficult human relationships.

God is important to Bobby. He says it's God who got him through his accident and it's God who is there for him in prison. He goes to chapel there. He sometimes forgets God when he's on the outside but he has faith that somehow it's God who's going to help him find his way out of the kind of troubled life he's leading. And he does want out of his kind of life.

For a week or two before he broke in here he was telling his substance abuse counselor and a social worker that his life was getting out of hand and he needed help. He says, "They kept telling me I was doing fine. They just looked at the outside and wouldn't look at what was going on inside." Bobby is not really able to say why he broke in here but it sounds to me like a cry for help, an attempt to make something happen in an intolerable situation.

Let me read you some excerpts from letters Bobby has written me while in jail.

"Pam, let me tell you that every time I think about the bad thing I've done I get mad at myself." "You know what, Pam, if only at the time I knew that people like you did like me, I would not get in as much trouble as I do, for I have been crying out for love. You know what? I'm glad I got caught. I like what you said in your letter about making it and I keep thinking to myself "Yes, I can make it, if I keep sticking around with people like you and Kathy. I see how the other way doesn't work. Pam, I've been thinking about what you said about me maybe being able to work around the church to pay back for the windows and I would be willing to do so even when I get done doing however much time I have to do."

"Pam, you know what? It sure is a good feeling knowing that when you come up to visit me you do it from the heart 'cause you want to and not 'cause you have to, for you see, all my life people did things for me 'cause they had to and let me tell you, they let me know it in a lot of ways."

So, is Bobby good or bad, deserving or undeserving? Should I be spending my time visiting him or would my time be better spent with someone who shows more promise of being able to become a self-sufficient, law-abiding citizen? I don't know the answer to those questions, nor I expect do most of you.

Bobby's a real person, a complicated human being. And while I grant that society must decide whether he's guilty or not and what his punishment is to be, we don't have to decide if he's good or bad, if he deserves our help or not. We're called to love him because he's the child of God. Whatever else he is, Christ dwells in him and we are called to minister to Christ.

How often have we heard "Judge not, lest ye be judged?" And yet I still hear all too many comments in relationship to Advent House, such as:

"If they can spend their money on alcohol and cigarettes they shouldn't be coming here."

"Anyone will take a free lunch,"

"Their only problem is that they lack ambition."

"They just need to learn to manage money better."

"They just need to clean up after themselves."

We want to reduce people to simple formulas and it doesn't work. Dirk Ficca, the Pastor of the Presbyterian Church in Benton Harbor, has done a lot of jail ministry and he's found there are eight givens in the lives of most inmates. They come from backgrounds of poverty, broken homes, substandard educational systems, they've been abused as children, they're minorities, they're addicted, they were unemployed or underemployed and they're incarcerated without rehabilitation.

And yet we insist on seeing people through our eyes when most of us have experienced only maybe one or two or three of those eight givens. We think people should be like us.

That's what Jesus was getting at with the parable of the Pharisee and the tax collector. When we look at people and say they should be like us we're also saying "Thank God I'm not like them." Jesus doesn't talk about needing to motivate the lazy, improve the IQ of the racially inferior, develop the underdeveloped, or control the demographic explosion of the excessively prolific. He does talk a lot about hypocrisy and self-righteousness.

Jesus came to proclaim "Good news to the poor, freedom for the prisoners, liberation for the oppressed." And we're called to do the same. It's not up to us to decide if people deserve our love or not—that's up to God. Why burden ourselves with another decision in a world when we already have too many decisions to make? We have plenty of work to do in following our calling. We're called to love, and that's enough.

Pam with her friend Marilyn. Michigan ordination 1987

Reflections from the top of a mountain

Psalm 95, Luke 6:12-19, Isaiah 42:10-16

September 4, 1988

We were almost to the top of the mountain. We'd been backpacking for a week in the Wind River Mountains in Wyoming with a group of fourteen of my family and friends. The climb on this particular day was the hardest yet. We had clambered over fields of boulders. I had fallen three times as rocks gave way under my feet. Most of us had slipped many times. Save for a small but treacherous piece at the top we had only a short walk up a glacier in order to reach our goal. It was a warm day and the glacier was slippery because of melting snow. The members of our group adopted various methods of glacier climbing. Some clasped hands pulling and sliding up the slush. Others adopted the solitary method of climbing on all fours. With no hands nearby to clasp, my friend, Marilyn Marshall, adopted the solitary method of climbing the glacier. She traversed, however, on two legs, digging her feet in sideways with each step. She was only a couple of steps from the top and was feeling quite pleased with her snow stomping accomplishment when she fell. Suddenly she found herself sliding down the glacier propelled by the weight of her pack. After some failed attempts she succeeded in bringing herself to a stop and there seated in cold, very wet snow, she cried.

It had been a lonely painful climb up to this point. My kids and their spouses are a naturally competitive bunch and most of them secretly desired to reach the top first and it showed in their hiking. Each one forged ahead in eager anticipation of triumph— until Marilyn fell, then we became community.

Leslie, my daughter, Bob, my son, and Bert, my brother-in-law scrambled down the glacier to help. Leslie took Marilyn's pack while Bert, reassuringly hugged her, then Bob and Bert each took a hand supportively and the three of them trudged safely up the glacier. The rest of us waited with concern until the three reached the top. There on the glacier God broke through our competiveness and made us all one.

God was present with us on that mountain. God was present in making us community and God was also present in the lives of individuals.

As a mother, I was particularly impressed and overwhelmed with the God that showed through in my youngest son, Bob. Bob is a sometimes-delightful college student who demonstrates both the exuberance and insecurity of a little boy and also the compassion and sensitivity of a young man. He's the kid who claimed he was matriphobic in order to avoid sharing a tent with his mother. But he's the one who hung back at the end of our group when he knew I was hurting, even though as a rule he always led the pack.

Once when I needed a hand up he was there to offer it. When I thanked him, he responded matter of factly and yet a bit awkwardly, "that's what friends are for." I saw a lot of God in Bob that day. God came through in his kindness and friendship. God was present with us on that mountain.

One of the people in our group who has a hard time believing in God was perhaps the one who showed us the most God of all. She was intentional about the way she spent her time in the group. She sought out individuals, asked them questions about themselves, and then gave herself over completely to listening and caring about what was being shared. Each of us felt very special and very cared for through her acts of ministry to us. I found myself breaking into an uncontrollable smile as I watched her reach out to each person in a genuine unpretentious way. I chuckled inwardly as I realized that though she may not profess belief in God, it is overwhelmingly apparent that God believes in her.

God was present with us on that mountain.

And God was present with each of us in our own personal struggles. My struggle revolved around the issue of declining physical ability. I was the oldest person in the group and so I expected to have trouble keeping up with the rest. But I didn't anticipate just how much trouble I'd have. On past trips I'd always been the one who brought up the rear, so that was okay and expected. There were some others who sometimes liked to hang back with me in "the slow group" as we were originally called. We later changed our group names from "slow group" and "fast group" to "Brains" and "Brawn"—those of us in the "Brains" group claiming we were smarter because we took the time to enjoy ourselves and God's creation all around us. But the thing that was different this year is that I'd always before been able to carry a 40 to 50 pound pack. This time it was obvious that I couldn't. It was bad enough that I couldn't carry some of the group equipment, but for a couple of days I couldn't even carry my own sleeping bag. That hurt! I pride myself on being strong and competent and able to do my share. I learned a lesson those days in the mountains that has been taught to me before, and will undoubtedly need to be taught to me again. That is that I am not in control of my life, God is. I learned again that God gives us different gifts, that God gives some the gift of greater strength and endurance and that it's okay to let those people help me when I need it. As I've grown older and lost physical strength I've gained in organizational and other support skills that are necessary to keep a group moving. I didn't have to be all things. I was part of a group—of community—created by God to be more than anyone of us could by ourselves.

God was present with us on that mountain. God WAS present with us on the mountain. I don't know why it is that God feels more accessible to me in the mountains but Jesus must have felt it too. Again and again, the gospels tell of Jesus retreating to the mountains to pray. When I'm in the mountains, living itself feels like praying.

Maybe it's because mountains are the most grand and flamboyant of God's creation. Maybe it's because mountains are so old that they bring us in touch with a sense of God's permanence. Maybe it's because they're so big, solid and unmovable that they help us get in touch with our God who is the "Rock of Ages."

One night when we camped above the timberline, we were surrounded on three sides by sheer walls of granite that touched the sky in sharp castle-like formations. They were beautiful in an eerie and foreboding, haunting kind of way. The first line of Luther's hymn, "A Mighty Fortress Is Our God" kept playing in my head as I experienced the power of those mountains. One could almost feel fearful of the God in those mountains. I've never related well to the parts of the Bible that talk about fearing God because I've always experienced God as a loving, comforting presence. But confronted with a God who made such mountains, a God who is so powerful, awe-inspiring, unmovable and unchangeable, I began to better understand the experience of that fear.

The overwhelming effect of these mountains is to make one feel small and insignificant. One member of our group said that being out in the mountains blanketed by a sky of brilliant starts causes her to wonder about the meaning of life; and to wonder if we are just random happenings. While I feel small in the mountains and less in control, I feel I am an integral, connected part of God's creation and my response is to praise God with the prophet Isaiah "Sing to the Lord a new song, God's praise from the end of earth … let them shout from the top of the mountains." And I do.

God was present in our wonderings. God was present with us on that mountain.

Now you may be wondering where the sermon is going. I've claimed God as present in a number of reasonably ordinary events. There were no big miracles on that mountain. There were no life and death encounters, and there were no Damascus road experiences, but there were miracles—the miracle of community, the miracle of different gifts, and the miracle of creation. There I go again—naming God's presence in day-to-day events.

You may ask how I know it is God at work in community and individuals and nature. The answer is that I don't know in any empirical sense—I know because through the Spirit I experience healing, love and wholeness by sharing in community, receiving individuals gifts, and participating in God's creation and these are of God.

God does come to us in ordinary day-to-day events, but it's easier to find God in those events on a mountain. Our vision is not obstructed as it is down here.

Jesus often went to the mountains to pray. In our scripture for today we hear of Jesus choosing his twelve disciples on the mountain after a night of prayer. Mountains are good places to make decisions. We need our mountains. We need our mountains whether they're physical or symbolic. We need the places where we retreat for a clearer perspective, for silence, and for waiting on God. We need places where it's easier to find God.

What are the places where you go to find God? I hope you've been there this summer. I hope God's presence has touched you in your day-to-day living. If you haven't been to a mountain, either physically or symbolically, go there. Go to the place where you find God even in the midst of pain, even in the midst of struggle, and most of all, even in the midst of ordinary events.

But after you've been there, come down. After we've been there, we have to come down. Jesus knew that. After he'd been on the mountain, he came down. "He came down…and stood on a level place." He came down to be with the people and to heal them of their diseases. And our scripture says "power came forth from him." We gain power on the mountain—power we're called upon to use when we come down from the mountain—power to be a healing presence to those we touch, power to engage in ministry to a broken world.

And so friends, let us give thanks to God who is present in all things: in community, in gifts and struggles, in nature and in mountains. And let us give thanks to God who not only leads us to the mountain, but also calls us down the mountain to ministry, and promises to always, always be with us.

Thanks be to God.

Pam with her children Bob, Leslie, A.A., Sue and Annie backpacking in Wyoming 1988

Beware

Exodus 3:1-15, Psalm 103: 1-13, 1 Corinthians 10:1-13, Luke 13: 1-9

February 26, 1989

I need to start with a confession. I do not like either our epistle lesson or our gospel lesson. In fact, I don't like many of the Lenten lectionary readings. They're filled with talk of sin and repentance, judgment, damnation and temptation. I don't much like dealing with any of those topics.

I suppose partly I don't want to deal with these topics because it's simply uncomfortable to deal with my own sin and guilt. I really don't want to hear that unless I repent I'll perish. I don't want to hear that I won't be tempted beyond my ability to endure it, for I don't want to be tempted at all. I really don't want to hear that I have only another year to bear good fruit before I am cut down. William Letty, a Presbyterian pastor in Scranton, Pennsylvania, apparently reacts to the fig tree account as I do. He's written a poem about it. Listen---

Lent III—On cutting the fig tree

*"…If it bears fruit next year, well and good;
but if not, you can cut it down" (Luke 13:9)*

When it is the fig tree,
Or the old prune tree in the hedgerow,
Or the sweet cherry tree the robins beat me to each summer:
I will agree to your timetable, and even help sharpen the saw.

But when it is a child of mine
Whose productivity is in question, whose laziness I know,
I want more time before the child is cut off.
Yes, I know there must be limits to the largesse,
Otherwise we aid and abet the fruitlessness.
But, to cut him off may be to lose the child. I fear.

When it is the fig tree in the orchard,
Yes, bring the double-edge axe sharpened for the test next year.
But, when it is the only industrial plant in town, the one employer, obsolete
and less productive than the standard,
I beg more time on behalf of workers.
I appeal a stay for owners and operators and the town.

When it is the fig tree,
And not my friend's fruitless, dried-up marriage…
When it is the fig tree,
Let us cut it after a fruitless year.
And you and I will take our ends of the crosscut, and split and season the logs,
And spend a winter's evening 'round the fire.
And in the flame of the then-burning bush,
I will hope to see you and to hear your voice.

None of us likes to hear hard things, but that's not the only reason I don't like these texts. I know perfectly well that sometimes we have to hear hard things. I also shy away from these texts because I think living a guilt-filled life is not a healthy way to live. Neither is it healthy to live in fear of the vengeance of God.

It's better, I think, to live a life grounded in grace and love and the knowledge that God cares for us and thinks we are each special and unique. It seems to me that when we are filled with love, that love spills over to loving our neighbors and we do good because we love, not because we're trying to avoid God's wrath. It seems to me that when we are filled with love we want to do the things that are right and healthy for ourselves and others and we don't have to worry much about temptation. That's my ideal anyway—and I believe that's the way it is in the Kingdom of God. I'm also forced to admit that the Kingdom is not yet, and the world is less than perfect, and that most of us are so damaged by a lack of love that we cannot open ourselves enough to God to be filled up with divine love. So perhaps in this imperfect world there is a place for warnings about sin and temptation.

One of the arguments in favor of always preaching from the lectionary texts is that it forces the preacher to deal with texts that she or he would ordinarily pass over. However, I'm willing to try to deal with those nasty topics not only because the lectionary includes them, but because I know that I can't define God the way I'd like to. The God of our faith is also a God of judgment. God's name, our old Testament text tells us is "I am who I am." That name can also be translated as "I will be what I will be." Neither are particularly helpful in giving us a good, clear, definitive picture of who God is.

I think perhaps the reason I have so much trouble understanding God as judge is because we mortals keep trying to cut God down to our size. When we think of God as judge we think of human judges, or of the way we judge individually, and we know that those judgments are often less than just.

God's judgment means the elimination of all that is evil. The only way we can conceive of that happening is through the destruction and dissolution of all beings who have been distorted by the evil in our world, and we know that we all stand under that judgment. But God is who God is and God can do things in ways we cannot imagine. Judgment is the flip side of grace and both are activities of a righteous God. Theologian William Macquarrie says "Belief in a judgment which is not merely ongoing but is also final, in the sense that it is a transforming of evil into good, a healing of injuries, a restoring of what has been destroyed or blighted, is an inevitable consequence of the belief that there is a righteous God, or that (God) is gracious."

When we think of sin, and try to list the things that calls forth God's judgment we're inclined to go to a Pauline list of things we're warned against, such as this from Colossians: fornication, impurity, passion, evil desire, covetous anger, wrath, malice, slander, and foul talk from your mouth. When I read a list like that I have a hard time relating to it and I suspect you may too. Certainly, I haven't seen this congregation suffering from an overdose of passion or evil desire, or of wrath or slander—I'll leave you to speculate about some of the others.

One thing I've found I like about our texts is that they warn us away from sins that you and I are more likely to succumb to. Our gospel text warns us away from self-righteousness, from assuming that we will be saved when others are punished. Our epistle counsels us to beware of presuming our status before God and others, and to be sensitive to beliefs and practices through which other folk perceive that which is holy.

Despite the warnings, how often are we tempted to think that we are better than other folks? How often do we assume that God loves us better because we go to church or do good deeds or simply don't do bad things? How often do we put down the practices of other faith traditions? If these things aren't very obvious to you, let me give you an example from my own life. I have a hard time dealing with the very fundamentalist churches which seem to be gaining in strength so rapidly these days. If I don't watch myself I find myself certain that I am right and they are wrong and think surely God must think so too. I often find myself making sarcastic remarks about them and their style of worship and preaching. But God warns me not to think those thoughts and say those things.

In his book "Taking Flight," Anthony de Mello tells the following tale which speaks to the kind of sin church folk often succumb to. Let me tell it to you:

> The priest announced that Jesus Christ himself was coming to church the following Sunday. People turned up in large numbers to see him. Everyone expected him to preach, but he only smiled when introduced and said, "Hello." Everyone offered him hospitality for the night, especially the priest, but he refused politely. He said he would spend the night in church. How fitting, everyone thought.
>
> He slipped away early next morning before the church doors were opened. And, to their horror, the priest and people found their church had been vandalized. Scribbled everywhere on the walls was the single word "Beware." No part of the church was spared: the doors and windows, the

pillars and the pulpit, the alter, even the Bible that rested on the lectern. "Beware." Scratched in large letters and in small, in pencil and pen and paint of every conceivable color. Wherever the eye rested one could see the words: "BEWARE, beware, Beware, Beware, beware, beware…" Shocking. Irritating. Confusing. Fascinating. Terrifying. What were they supposed to beware of? It did not say. It just said "Beware." The first impulse of the people was to wipe out every trace of this defilement, this sacrilege. They were restrained from doing this only by the thought that it was Jesus himself who had done this deed.

Now that mysterious word "Beware" began to sink into the minds of the people each time they came to church. They began to beware of the Scriptures, so they were able to profit from the Scriptures without falling into bigotry. They began to beware of sacraments, so they were sanctified without becoming superstitious. The priest began to beware of his power over the people, so he was able to help without controlling. And everyone began to beware of religion which leads the unwary to self-righteousness. They became law-abiding, yet compassionate to the weak. They began to beware of prayer, so it no longer stopped them from becoming self-reliant. They even began to beware of their notions of God so they were able to recognize God outside the narrow confines of their church.

They have now inscribed the shocking word over the entrance of their church and as you drive past at night you can see it blazing above the church in multicolored neon lights.

How about you? Of what do you need to beware? Of self-righteousness or bigotry? Of wanting to control others or conversely of needing to be too dependent? Of legalism? Of the idolatry of trying to define God for yourself?

We don't really know what God's judgment means or how it will get played out. So in the meantime, perhaps we'd do well to listen to the warnings and beware.

Thanks be to God.

Journey in the spirit

Acts 2:1-21; John 15:26-27, 16:4b-15

May 22, 1994

The disciples had the experience of seeing Jesus. They knew that work remained for them to do. They had elected a new disciple to take the place of Judas. But still they were waiting, wondering what would happen to them, to the Jesus movement that had started when Jesus was with them. Jesus had told Peter he was founding his church upon him. But now what should Peter do? What should any of them do? They waited. They wondered.

We, the disciples of today, the followers of Jesus at Westminster Presbyterian Church know that Jesus lives. We know that Jesus has given us work to do. We know what his commands are, but our life together in Jesus has sometimes seemed cloudy and our direction less clear than it used to. Our church has suffered through a major controversy, leaving some with bad feelings and a bitter taste. Our numbers and our dollars are dwindling. I am leaving and to some the future shape of this church's ministry is uncertain. Phil has cancer and his future is unclear. Outside of this dear building the violence increases and much that we knew about life as sure and certain, crumbles like a sand castle on a beach.

Many of you are here this morning to honor and welcome and congratulate our young people who are being confirmed. Many of you come because it's my last time to preach and you want to say "Good-bye." Some of you come out of habit or because it seems that you're supposed to. But I think, and know it's true for me, that in the back of our minds there's always the hope that something will happen in worship—that something will happen that will assure us that God is present and in control. So in a sense we, like the early disciples, come to watch and wait.

Something did happen for the disciples who gathered on this day so long ago. There came a sound of the rush of a mighty wind that filled all the house. Then came tongues of fire resting on each of them. And the Holy Spirit filled them and they were able to speak in the languages of all around them. Peter reminded them of the prophecy of Joel: "I will pour out my Spirit on all flesh, and your sons and your daughters will prophecy, and your young men will see visions and your old men will dream dreams…I will show the wonders of heaven and signs on the earth…And it shall be that whoever calls on the name of the Lord shall be saved."

We, here, gathered in this place call on the name of the Lord. And we wait for something to happen.

But we have something the first disciple didn't have. We have memory of more than just a prophecy. We have memory of a Spirit-filled church. We have memory of what it is like to live by the direction of the Spirit. We can give the witness of faith and share our experiences of God's power, presence and love while we wait for new experiences of the Spirit and new directions for life together in this community of faith.

One of the functions of the Spirit is to help us remember. Much of what we do in church is remember our history and our Lord. Indeed, in the mystery of communion, we, with the Spirit's help, recall "…on the night in which he was betrayed." We remember his passion and his death, his resurrection and his ascension. The very life and mission of the church depends on memory. So, since it's Pentecost and since this is my last time to preach to you, I want to do some remembering.

When I think of Spirit-filled times in this church I think of Pentecost 1988. I had been here for a year and a half but somehow had never baptized anyone in that time. On that Pentecost Sunday we had a bunch of baptisms, I don't remember exactly how many. There were children and young people of varying ages from an American family, Mao Her's family and a Korean family that was here and part of our life for a year or two. Ed remembers being embarrassed that day because he was helping our young people paint Casa del CONA, our first shelter home. Ed came to church and sat in the balcony because he was in paint clothes, but Phil called him down to be part of the baptisms along with Margaret Groves because they had worked with Mao's family. Ed and I had dated a few times but until that point neither of us were sure we really wanted to pursue the relationship much further. Somehow that day it felt very right that Ed should be standing there with me. That morning felt to me like the church was meant to be. It was a beautiful May morning, clear and warm, hot even, and with all the new Christians of different races and nationalities, it felt like Pentecost of old. I could almost feel the rush of wind and flash of fire. I knew the Spirit had crashed in upon us here in this sanctuary.

That afternoon work continued on the painting of Casa del CONA. When I came to Lansing churches didn't do many things together, even within denominations, much less across denominations. That Sunday was a first. Our youth group had joined together with those from Delta Presbyterian Church and Holy Cross Catholic Church to do the painting. There was a good group of young people, and a sense of purpose and accomplishment, and good feelings about each other. One of the fruits of the Spirit that has dwelt in this place has been the development of good ecumenical relationships—churches working together in service in the name of Jesus Christ. You, as a congregation, pushed me hard to build those relationships when I first came. That was your vision and the Spirit working through you and through me that accomplished it.

When the painting was done on that Pentecost of 1988, Ed brought in 18 paintbrushes that needed cleaning, and he and I stood at the kitchen sink downstairs, cleaning paintbrushes and fell in love. I'm not sure that was the fruit of the Spirit, but perhaps it was.

I contrast my remembrances of the Spirit's work in this church with a statement I found in a publication I get which offers help to pastors in sermon preparation. This is what it says: "You know the problem. Our claim to have received the Spirit is not substantiated in our living. The gift of the Spirit produces no life or community very different from others. Society looks to sources of help other than the church even when seeking some sort of 'spirituality.' In concrete problems of hunger, hate, and oppression, the church is either incompetent or complacent. Communities that have no churchly connection often have more active regard for the poor than does the church."

"Not true, not true," I wanted to shout at the author. I will acknowledge that we're not always what we should be. We have been and can be hateful with one another. But, my friends, we've been good too. And I defy anyone to say this church has no concern for the poor. People know this church by its commitment to the poor and its concern for ministries of caring.

The story that keeps coming back to me that somehow wants to be told again is that of Bobby Trevino. Some of you will remember that Bobby, a not very bright, alcoholic, habitual offender, regular Advent House guest was caught by police dogs in our building one night in 1987. He had stolen two bags of groceries. Phil and I tried to get the authorities to drop charges, but they wouldn't. Because Bobby Trevino was poor and not smart and had a record, he was not brought to trial for an entire year. During that year Cathy Sanchez, a social worker at Cristo Rey and I visited Bobby regularly and our visits were important to him. He wrote us lots of letters and painted pictures for us. When Christmas came I urged you, the congregation, to send him Christmas Cards and notes of support. You did. Lots of you did. Bobby had never experienced anything like that before and he wrote that it was his "best Christmas ever." Bobby has stayed out of jail since then. He's living in a group home which is where he should have been all along. He comes by to visit periodically. This church is important to him. People in this church cared for Bobby even though they didn't know him, even though he had committed a crime against them, and they gave him his "best Christmas ever."

I think of another woman many of you know. She'll need to remain nameless to those of you who don't know her. She's a woman with seven children. We first met her in 1987 when she came to live in Casa del CONA. She worked in the Bake Shop for a while, but really wasn't able to do the work because of learning disabilities. She's been homeless several times since we've known her. Some of her kids have been taken away because she simply hasn't the ability to keep a clean house or control her children, even though she loves them deeply. She's used every program Advent House has again and again. She has come to church at times. Her kids have attended Sunday school at times. Nothing changes for her. She's still here. We don't win them all. In fact, we don't win most of them. You know how I keep saying to you that we are not called to be successful, we're called to be faithful. We've been faithful. Those of you who have known this woman have been unfailingly gracious and kind and caring. And no one in the secular world has given her that kind of love.

There is a new baker in the Bake Shop. She had learned about the Bake Shop through a human resource guide and thought it might be a place she could get the kind of help she needed, but she didn't act on it then. Some weeks later, she heard about it at an agency fair at the YWCA and thought maybe God wanted her to call us. She did and when she arrived here for her appointment with Chris, she found a sign on the front door saying "The door is open" and that sign said to her that God was opening a door for her.

That's the way the Spirit manifests itself in this church. Even though we have to have locks on our doors and sophisticated alarm systems, somehow this door is always open and hearts are open and arms are open.

I could go on remembering things that have happened here over the last seven years for a long time but we have much to do yet this morning. We have yet to say "Good-bye." We need to say "Hello" to our new Christians and new members of this church. We need to remember our Lord in the sacrament of Communion. But I hope that after I leave, you will keep remembering the ministry we have done here together and let it give shape and meaning to your life together in the future. And listen for the rush of wind. Look for the tongues of fire. Wait for the Spirit as did the disciples of old. Be ready to receive the Spirit when it comes. For it will come.

Pam and Ed on their wedding day 1989

A Sanctuary for childhood

Matthew 18:1-7

September 17, 1995

When my oldest daughter Anna returned from a month in Germany a couple of weeks ago she stopped on her way home to see her younger sister Susan, the mother of my four-year-old granddaughter Megan. Anna brought Sue a present from Germany of some fancy glassware which was on the table at dinnertime. As dinner began Megan said "Let's do cheers," meaning let's make a toast. Sue said "Okay, who do you want to toast?" And Megan said "Let's toast God" and then she thought again and said, "No, Let's toast Santa Claus." A cute story—yes. I laughed when I heard it. But upon reflection it seemed symbolic of what's happening to our children, indeed to our culture.

You may remember that in our last newsletter I said a majority of our country still identifies itself as Christian. Well, I just saw figures that say that's no longer true. A majority of people in this country now say they are non-Christian or have no religion. And to restate something I said in the newsletter, only 25% of our people are active Christians. I assumed that meant that one of four kids in the schools go to church, but Ellyn Plackowski says she believes it's more like one in ten, and I guess if you look at all the gray heads in our churches that may be true.

Our children's friends, and I use the word "our" to mean my kids, the children of this church, your kids and grandkids and great-grandkids, wherever they are—our children's friends put them down for going to church. Often our kids don't want others to know they go to church. Other kids tell them church is boring or stupid, that they're being programmed to believe something that isn't true. It's hard for a kid to claim to be a Christian.

Our kids are growing up in a culture that is totally different from the one in which we grew up. The old social contract with which we grew up has been broken. We live today in an age of instant gratification. Daniel Yankelovich, in a book written back in 1981 says this of the social contract, which he calls the giving/getting compact:

"The old giving/getting contract might be paraphrased this way: I give hard work, loyalty and steadfastness. I swallow my frustrations and suppress my impulses to do what I would enjoy, and do what is expected instead. I do not put myself first; I put the needs of others ahead of my own. I give a lot, but what

I get in return is worth it. I receive an ever-growing standard of living and a family life with a devoted spouse and decent kids. Our children will take care of us in our old age if we really need it, which thank goodness we will not. I have a nice home, a decent job, the respect of my friends and neighbors; a sense of accomplishment at having made something of my life."(1)

That's what we grew up with. Not so different from the Christian message in many ways, is it? The Christian message puts a high value on sacrificing now and enjoying the rewards of eternal life. The Christian message puts a high value on putting others first and ourselves last. The Christian message puts a high value on community and the equality of all God's people. The Christian message, at least as interpreted by Protestantism, certainly put a high value on work.

But what is it like for our kids? This is the age of credit cards, of instant gratification, this is the age when Santa Claus is better than God. The need for ever-increasing consumer spending is what drives our economy. We are urged to buy and buy and spend and spend and we are told there is no need to wait, no need to save. If you want it now, you should have it.

At the same time there is no assurance that we will have ever increasing incomes. Real wages have gone down 16% between 1985 and 1993. Medicare is under attack and it may well be that our children will have to take care of us in old age, if they have the money. We no longer can count on having a loving, faithful spouse—50% of marriages made these days don't last. We moved from an era where saving and working hard and responsibility and loyalty were paramount in the thirties and forties to the boom era of the fifties with the advent of credit cards to the "now" generation of the 60s where what we heard was "if it feels good, do it" then to "Me" generation of the 70s and the "Greed" generation of the 80s. Who knows what the 90s will be called but I don't think it's going to be any more flattering.

Is it any wonder that the Christian message with its emphasis on sacrifice and putting others first makes no sense to people raised in this generation? Is it any wonder that kids today think that what they hear in that one half hour of Sunday School a week is stupid?

Another thing that's been happening is an increased emphasis on rights of the individual as opposed to obligations to family or community. Let me read another quote, this time from a parent, about another way in which the old social contract has broken down.(2)

"Where I grew up, if I misbehaved I could be reprimanded by anyone in town and I knew my parents would stand behind whatever was said. Neighbors and shopkeepers and teachers and ministers had a kind of covenant to work together to help bring children up right. I moved away from that town, grateful to be out from under too many eyes and ears and noses. Even though I was glad for the freedom, I have often said I was raised by my community. Today, I don't know my neighbors and I don't dare criticize my children's friends. The covenant has been broken, and we are not better off. I am tired of hearing about what families and parents are doing or not doing for their children as if every social ill were all our fault. We have to figure out a way to get the covenant back…"

Our children are threatened. They are threatened by a culture that says work is not important. What's important is having fun now. Having money now. Having things now. They are threatened by families who are too busy working, or too busy drinking to have enough time to know what their kids are doing. They are threatened by a society that doesn't see other peoples' kids as their responsibility. They are threatened by a lack of a future. They are threatened by child abuse and alcohol and drugs and sex.

We have a serious problem in this community that I don't see anybody addressing. There are a number of young men, mostly out of high school, between the ages of 18 and 25 who are preying on our sixth and seventh grade girls. They pick up the girls downtown after school and take them into the woods or to someone's home, give them alcohol, introduce them to hard drugs, and then gang rape them and sometimes do things worse than that. And these are not just a few of the "bad" girls from "bad" families. They are little girls looking for someone to love them. Estimates are that about half of our 11 to 13 year olds are involved. The police are trying to do something about it but it's hard to get the evidence they need. Why won't the families press charges? What has happened to the neighbors and people who, seeing a child get in a car with men ten years older than she is, would call that child's parents? What has happened to the Dads who in days gone by would have said "I'm going to kill him" about anyone who raped their daughters? Now they just say "We don't want any more trouble." I've heard rumbles about this problem since I've been here. Why isn't anyone doing anything about it? Why aren't people talking about it? Why are we all burying our heads in the sand?

And Jesus says "If anyone of you put a stumbling block before one of these little ones who believe in me, it would be better for you if a great millstone were fastened around your neck and you were thrown into the depth of the sea. Woe to the world because of stumbling blocks."

The central Christian story begins with the birth of a child. In the birth of the Christ child, God took on all the powerlessness, weakness, and neediness of human childhood for the sake of our salvation. What is remarkable about that story is that the truth of God is embodied in a child. It is the child who carries in himself or herself the hope of the world.

The church has always been committed to welcoming children. The invitation of Jesus to "Let the children come" permanently expanded the membership of the people of God. The church today is called to do what Jesus did: to welcome the children in order to bless them. The church must become a sanctuary for childhood, sanctuary in the sense of being a safe harbor in an unsafe world, a place that is community where children are welcomed and honored as fully human and where there is compassion and justice for all persons. The church that offers children sanctuary, will welcome children as full participants in the life of God's people; it will support parents in their ever-changing roles, the spiritual formation of children will have new direction and urgency. The church which offers sanctuary for children will intervene when children or families experience extraordinary problems and needs; and the church will advocate for systemic change where families are endangered; and it will challenge individuals, families, and society to a deepening regard for children as the measure of God's justice and mercy in the world.

I've run out of time. I'd like to be specific about this church and how we welcome our children and how this church might become a sanctuary for our own children, but perhaps it's not for me to say. It's for all of us in this community of faith to come together, to look our problems squarely in the eye, and to pray together, to talk together, to act together to save our children, to offer them sanctuary.

24 *Wisdom and politics*

God help us all.

1. *New Rules, Searching for Self-Fulfillment in a World Turned Upside Down*, by Daniel Yankelovich (Random House, 1981)
2. *Regarding Children: A New Respect for Childhood and Families*, by Herbert Anderson & Susan W. Johnson (Westminster: John Know Press, 1994)

Ed and Pam with Faith, Chastity, and Jimmy Morgan

Homosexuality, the Bible, and the Church

Acts 10, Galatians 3:23-29

June 30, 1996

I have not wanted to conceal or camouflage the concern upon which we will be focusing this morning. Hence, the candid sermon title: "Homosexuality, the Bible and the Church." But before I get into it, I'd like you to know, not only what this sermon is about, but why I am preaching it. In 1975 a young man, under the care of the Presbytery of New York presented his final parts of trial for ordination to the ministry in the Presbyterian Church. His exegesis, sermon and statement of faith were judged to be well done. A lifelong Presbyterian, he presented impressive potential for Christian leadership in the judgment of the Candidates Committee. He offered moving testimony of repentance from sin and acceptance of Jesus Christ as Lord and Savior. He also affirmed that he was homosexual and that his lifestyle was responsible and loving and therefore not sinful. The Candidates Committee was uncertain whether this last view was compatible with the Form of Government of the Presbyterian church. The Candidates Committee believed this was a critical issue which needed to be addressed by the whole church. As a consequence the General Assembly, our national governing body, appointed a task force to study "Christian approaches to homosexuality." In 1978, after receiving the report of its task force, the General Assembly rejected one of the key recommendations and declared that the ordination of "unrepentant" homosexuals as ministers, elders, and deacons is inappropriate. According to this decision, it does not matter if people are in every other respect fit for ordination, if they are homosexual and if they are honest about it, they are disqualified. At the same time, the General Assembly urged the church to welcome homosexual persons of faith into membership. And the Assembly went on to condemn the "sin" of homophobia; the treatment of gay and lesbian people with "contempt, hatred, and fear." Many people felt that there was inconsistency and self-contradiction in the General Assembly's statement. The debate over the issue has raged ever since. This year's General Assembly is meeting as we speak in Albuquerque and facing a significant vote on the ordination question after a three-year moratorium on consideration of all such questions. You will likely be hearing about it in the news.

    I believe that as your pastor you should have some idea where I stand on the issue and that is why I am choosing to deal with the topic of homosexuality today. Some of you will not like what I am going to say. I know that. I expect that. If after having heard me out you still have questions, concerns, or disagreements, be sure that I am ready to listen to you. This is a very divisive issue. As a result of the General Assembly's decision this week, some people and perhaps some churches will leave the denomination. I hope and expect that in this church we can converse in love and mutual respect.

Frankly, I would have preferred a different forum—one where questions might be asked and discussion might take place. In other words I'd rather do this in an adult education group than in a pulpit. But I felt I needed to reach as many of you as I could.

Whenever the issue of homosexuality is raised in the church, one of the first questions is: What does the Bible say? The answer is: not much. Homosexuality is not a great concern of the Scriptures.

In the Old Testament there is the story of Sodom and Gomorrah. But most scholars today find that story to an indictment, not of homosexuality, but of inhospitality. Wherever, in the rest of the Bible, there is a reference to the destruction of Sodom, it is in that vein. As in the case of Ezekiel, for example, who declares: "This was the guilt of your sister Sodom; she and her daughters had pride, surfeit of food and prosperous ease, but did not aid the poor and needy."

In the Book of Leviticus we are given a law prohibiting homosexual behavior on the part of males. Such behavior is labeled "an abomination." But those who like to use this text as an excuse for rejecting and even punishing homosexuals, fail to point out all the other things which the Levitical Code considers "abominations" which don't bother us at all. Eating pork, for instance, or cross-breeding cattle, or sowing two kinds of seed in the same field, or wearing a garment made from two kinds of fabric. According to Leviticus, if that coat or dress you're wearing today is a mixture of wool and cotton, you are in deep trouble.

All these prohibitions, which seem silly to us, appear in the Levitical Code for one reason. At the time, the Hebrew people were a tiny minority surrounded on all sides by pagan culture. They were concerned to preserve their identity as unique people of faith. And so, many things commonplace in non-Hebrew societies, including homosexual behavior, were prohibited. The question that has to be asked, is this: On what basis do Christians today ignore all these so-called "abominations" except one—the one concerning homosexuality?

As for the New Testament, Jesus is not reported to have said anything about the subject. He said a great deal, as you know, about various sins and temptations. He spoke about the dangers of wealth, about a judgmental and unforgiving spirit, about adultery, about pride and hypocrisy. If homosexuality were as great an evil as some say, one would think Jesus might have mentioned it. But he didn't.

Paul does speak to the issue. Again, however, it is not something that preoccupies him. Both the First Letter to the Corinthians and I Timothy include homosexual behavior in sin lists which also include idolaters, drunkards, greed, envy, strife, craftiness, gossips, slanderers and God-haters. As twentieth century Christians, the more responsible way to deal with those sin lists or vice lists that appear throughout the New Testament is to ask what new vices of our modern world might be added, rather than waging moral crusades against specific vices.

What's not clear at all for Christians today are the implications of the passage for a moral evaluation about caring, committed same-sex relationships. The idea of sexual orientation was unknown in Paul's world. It was assumed that everyone was naturally heterosexual. Now we know that matters are more complicated. Some people—estimates range from 5-10% of the population—are of homosexual orientation. That percentage is consistent across cultures and across species. Why this is so is not clear. But increasingly science is pointing to physical and genetic causes.

Paul seems to have assumed not only that homosexuality was "unnatural" —which we know now is not so. He also assumed that all homosexual behavior was exploitive and demeaning. Most homosexual behavior in the world Paul lived in was between older men and young boys. He seems not to have considered the possibility of caring adult homosexual relationships.

The major passage in which Paul condemns homosexuality is in Romans 1:26-27. While sexual behavior is clearly emphasized in the passage, Paul's major purpose is not to offer a sexual ethics for Christians.

The passage in which these verses appear is about the free grace offered to all through faith in Christ. The main argument of this passage is that all human beings stand equally before an impartial God. He argues the case by using traditional viewpoints (such as those about same-sex behavior) in a way which will be persuasive to his readers. But to focus exclusively on those viewpoints as his core ethical conviction is not to take the Bible seriously.

Ironically, this passage from Romans, which so many use to judge homosexuals, warns against human judgment of the sins listed there by insisting that judgment belongs only to God. Paul uses the stereotyped denunciations of the Gentile world not in order to talk about homosexuality, but to nail the self-righteous—be they heterosexuals or homosexuals.

Is the Bible, then, of no use to us in our effort to know how to respond to the issue of homosexuality? As Paul himself might say, by no means!

We need to remember that what we are dealing with is not just an issue—homosexuality—but with persons who happen, among other things to be homosexual. They are persons, first and foremost. And within the community of faith they are Christian persons. They trust Jesus Christ as Lord and Savior. They love his church as much as the rest of us. They are as morally sensitive as anybody else. Do they need forgiveness? Of course. Who doesn't? But what they don't need forgiveness for is who they are. What they need, as all of us do, is understanding and compassion—and a little help in their struggle for justice. For, homosexual people continue to experience hostility and discrimination. Some have been frozen out of their families. Many live in fear. All have experienced rejection.

The basic issue is how we treat our fellow human beings. And the Bible has a lot to say about what that means. "Beloved, let us love one another; for love is of God—Whoever does not love does not know God—if we love one another God abides in us, and his love is perfected in us—there is no fear in love, but perfect love casts out fear."

I chose the scripture passages for today for one reason, that being my conclusion, drawn from Scripture, that nothing is closer to the heart of Christ's gospel and nothing clearer from his own behavior than that his Kingdom includes rather than excludes. We modern Presbyterians are not the only ones to have fought over this kind of issue. The story of Peter and Cornelius is about a church fight, particularly about whether or not Gentiles (all people who weren't Jews) could be included in the church. Turn to Acts 11 and you'll see Peter defending himself for baptizing Gentiles. Peter was a Jew. For him it was forbidden to even sit down at the table with a Gentile, just as it was forbidden to eat of certain kinds of foods. Gentiles comprised a category of unclean person, just as pork was a category of unclean food. But a vision, perhaps even a conviction about Christ, leads him to change his mind. "I truly understand," Peter says "that God shows no partiality."

As for Paul, I think that what he has to say in Galatians has far more bearing on the issue of homosexuality and the church than the two or three obscure, very specific, references he makes to homosexual behavior. The purpose of Paul's letter to the Galatians is to say that it is our faith in Christ that makes us Christians. Nothing matters but our faith. "There is neither Jew nor Greek, there is neither slave or free, there is neither male or female, for you are all one in Christ Jesus."

Paul does not pretend that distinctions among people do not exist. He says that they don't matter. We could name a hundred things that make people different from one another: their color, their health, their wealth, their politics, their nationality, their age, their marital status, and their sexual orientation. But Paul is saying, whatever the differences among people, in the church they don't matter. "You are all one in Christ Jesus." You are all God's children and you are all in need of God's saving grace.

I long for the time when our denomination will catch up with Paul's understanding of church, as much as I long for the time when it will grow beyond Paul's understanding of homosexuality. As regards to ordination, I hope we can get to the point when, in deciding who should be ordained, we don't ask about a candidate's sexual orientation any more than we do about his or her wealth or occupation, or color, or age. I hope we can reach the point where we are concerned only with a person's faith, character, commitment, and wisdom.

The debate in the Presbyterian Church has been a painful one that raises questions which demand that we think carefully about who God is, who we are to God, how Scriptures should be interpreted, and what the church is all about. Gay and lesbian persons are our brothers and sisters, our neighbors and colleagues. We, like they, need the grace of Christ whose love abolishes barriers, tears down walls, and makes God's Kingdom a reality for all. I challenge you to pray, to read, to discuss. I challenge you to risk loving, for it is in loving, that God is found.

The Food at your door (Thanksgiving)

Isaiah 55:1-3a, II Corinthians 4:5-12

June 1, 1997

Once upon a time there was a man who woke up in the morning and found food outside his door. There was no hint of who had left the food or why. Naturally the man was pleased to find the food outside his door. The food that had been left for him was of the highest quality and of a far greater variety than he could possibly have hoped to provide for himself. Naturally the man was thankful. Although he did not know who had left the food, he thanked the open air for this generous gift, hoping that somehow his benefactor might hear his thanks. Naturally the man was curious. He wanted to find out who had left the food outside his door and why.

The next morning when the man awoke, once again he found food outside his door. And the next morning. And the next. His curiosity and his gratitude continued to grow until he determined that he would stay awake one night and discover who this caring person was who was so graciously providing for his needs. That evening he took a post by his front window where he could observe his front doorstep without himself being seen. But as fate would have it, there must have been an instant during the night that his vigilance waned, and he nodded off, if only for a moment. But in that moment his benefactor had managed to make an appearance and once again leave food at his door unseen. For many evenings the man tried to catch the mysterious giver, but the results were always the same—in a flash of inattention, he would miss the donor, and food would be anonymously at his door once again.

His desire to discover the source of his daily blessings became a driving force in the man's life. Not a day went by that the man did not silently thank whoever it was who was showing such care and faithfulness toward him. One day, in conversation with his neighbor, the man told his friend about the wonderful thing that had been happening to him each and every morning. Much to the man's surprise, his neighbor smiled and said, "Yes, I know—it's been happening to me, too." Whoever the man's benefactor was, he was providing gifts to his neighbor every bit as abundant and faithfully as his own. What a rich, caring person this stranger must be! The two decided to join forces in attempting to find the source of their blessing.

Their search did not last long. No, they didn't find out who was putting food at their door every morning. What they discovered was that each and every person they talked to was receiving exactly the same blessing they were receiving. Every single person in the village—indeed, every single person in the country, woke in the morning to find food at their door.

Then something happened. Where once upon a time the man felt particularly blessed and, because of that particular blessing, tremendously grateful, that sense of blessing quickly began to fade. Oh, the food was still there at his door every morning, just as bountiful and just as delicious, sometimes even more so, as the first day he had discovered it. That had not changed at all. But now the man no longer felt special. He no longer felt that whoever was doing this for him really cared about him. His thoughts no longer turned outward in gratitude toward the mysterious stranger and his unfailing gifts; his thoughts turned inward in greed and petulance. If he really cared about me, the man thought, the stranger wouldn't be giving so much to my neighbors. If he really cared about me, he wouldn't be giving anything to my neighbors. The man stopped saying his quiet thanks every morning when he discovered the food at his door. The man lost his curiosity about the giving stranger, and in a surprisingly short time, the man stopped thinking about the giving stranger altogether.

The most curious thing of all is that the food kept coming. Every morning the man would wake to find a beautiful array of food on his doorstep. Every day the man would enjoy the bounty presented to him, eating and drinking and living on the gifts left for him. Although he continued to receive, he never spent another moment of his life trying to discover the source of his abundance; he never spent another moment of his life wondering; he never spent another moment of his life in thanks.

When, after many, many years, the man had enjoyed his last meal and the life had finally left his body—as it must leave each of us—the mysterious giver noticed on his nightly visit that the man had not used the food he had left the day before. Quietly, the mysterious giver entered the house where he had never been. Silently, he touched the lifeless body that had grown to manhood and through adulthood, nourished by his unfailing gifts. And as he turned and passed through the doorway to begin the long walk home, the pale light of a dying candle on the nightstand lit the mysterious giver's face, and a tear that welled in the corner of his eye. The mysterious giver had wanted nothing more than to be a friend. But he remained forever a stranger.

Who do you thank for life? Or maybe I should put that question another way—do you thank anyone for life? Have you stopped lately to consider how special, how wonderful, how extraordinary your life is? Have you noticed the incredible array of creation laid out at your doorstep every morning? The sun in its course through the sky? The rains nourishing all growing things? The sights, the sounds, the smells, the feelings—so many of which are yours alone, shared by no one else on earth? Does the fact that others are also so blessed lessen the beauty of the gift you receive by one ounce? Should it? Do you search for the mysterious giver who blesses you so, or have you given up the effort to discover who he is and what he would like to be to you?

Crying in the wilderness

Isaiah 11:1-10, Matthew 3:1-12

December 6, 1998

Who is the one crying in the wilderness, and who will prepare the way of the Lord?

When I was a child I often felt very lonely. My mother was often depressed and was compulsively neat so she didn't like for me to have friends over very often because we made too much of a mess. She would often complain to me "Why can't you ever play by yourself?" We learned early not to talk about Mom's illness and to cover up for her. You might say that my mom lived in a wilderness of her depression and I also lived in a wilderness of trying to take care of my mother.

But at Christmas the real world ceased to exist. Mom liked Christmas and I was caught up in the promise: *You better watch out, you better not cry, you better not pout, I'm telling you why, Santa Claus is coming to town.* I knew Santa was making a list, so as soon as Thanksgiving was over, I started being good. I practiced smiling. I was nice to my little brother. As the mountain of packages began to grow under the tree, I very secretly and carefully began pinching and shaking the gifts addressed to me, trying to decide which gift would be the one I would choose to open after church on Christmas Eve. Boxes continued to arrive. Mom, who was not usually much into cooking, baked cookies and breads. Decorations went up and my brother and I spent hours putting icicles on the tree. My Dad insisted the tree be so coated in tinsel you could hardly see anything else. Other decorations went up and if there were any cares in the world outside, I wasn't aware.

In third grade my best friend was a little girl whose parents were Italian immigrants. I lived in a town with many immigrants from Italy and they all lived in the poor section of town and my mother said she really wished I'd find someone else to play with. But I loved to go to Priscilla's house. It was smaller and darker and messier than ours, but it was warm and noisy, and filled with colorful bottles and plants, and there were usually wonderful smells coming from the kitchen. Not long after the beginning of school Priscilla's father was injured at work and her mother took in ironing. I didn't think about it much.

As Christmas approached, both our houses began to glow with Christmas magic—lights, trees, cookies, breads. And yet as Christmas approached a nagging cloud seemed to develop and hang over our friendship. The presents under the tree at our house grew and spilled out into the room. Under my friend's tree were the small presents we made in school—not much more.

On Christmas Eve, just before we were leaving to go to church, Priscilla and her mother came to my house with a large cake and some candy and a little plant. My mother scrambled to put together a plate of cookies and breads—a small dent in our mountain of plenty. I cried that night and my father said I was becoming aware of the world around me—I was becoming aware of the wilderness and I wasn't sure that such awareness was a good thing.

Who is crying in the wilderness, and who will prepare the way for the Lord?

Later, in eighth grade, another best friend told me that she hated Christmas. Most of the time just her father drank, but at Christmas everyone drank. Things got broken, words were spoken, people's space and person were violated. At the time I chose not to become aware of the fear and the pain around me. Not that I didn't care. I just didn't know what to say or do. We had our worst fight just before Christmas and our friendship seemed shattered and peace on earth seemed like a cruel joke.

Who is the one crying in the wilderness, and who will prepare the way for the Lord?

As a young mother, I wanted to recreate the Christmas magic I felt as a child. In a time of Viet Nam, and civil rights riots and assassinations, we limited our conversation to love, giving, candy, presents, Santa, and the Christ child. Trying to create a world that was, just for a moment, close to the perfection that I thought God willed. I didn't want to see, and I didn't want my children to see, the awful reality of the world it was—not at Christmas.

Then came the year my five children and I entered the living room on Christmas morning to open presents. My second daughter Sue said "Someone's missing." And he was. My husband, their father, had left us a few months earlier and we were left with our perfect family Christmas vision in a shambles. Even the magic of Christmas couldn't erase the hurt, the fear, the anger, the betrayal. We were the ones crying in the wilderness. Who would prepare the way for the Lord?

There were several other wildernesses after that. The wilderness of teenage mothers, the wilderness of being a woman in ministry, the wilderness of homelessness, and most recently the wilderness of conflict in Israel. As I cried in the wilderness, what was being prepared? Why was John calling people to repent and be baptized? Why did John call the Pharisees and Sadducees, who came to repent and be baptized, a brood of vipers and unworthy of repentance?

I'm not sure I know the answer for others, but for myself I know that until I experienced my own personal wilderness, I just didn't get it. My heart knew to cry when my poor friend brought us a big Christmas cake, and my spirit was uneasy when my friend told me about the horrors of Christmas at her house. But to acknowledge poverty, abuse, loneliness, violence, and my own mother's illness, and to not know what to do to make it different, is to risk feeling powerless and incompetent.

The work of Christmas is not the lovely play of lights, good smells, presents, and food baskets for the poor. It is the work of risking to see each other as we really are—lonely, hurt, afraid, hungry, in need of love and forgiveness that God offers; and it is the work of risking to see the world as it really is—caught in the struggle for power, wealth, land, influence, votes—a world so caught up in the mechanics of survival that people, individuals, get overlooked and stepped on.

Advent means *parousia*—arrival, coming—it is both the present and the future. The Messiah whose advent we celebrate and expect is a reviver of the ancient promise to the Davidic dynasty. He is an agent of God's deliverance. He is the son of God who will come in the end times. He is a political, ethical savior. To understand or act on only one meaning of advent and the coming Messiah, is to be lost in the wilderness.

Many, like Judas, expected Jesus to be a political savior, the one who would lead the arm of Israel to conquer the Romans and return Israel to its rightful position in the world. But Christ accepts every applicant, and his army is full of rag-tag, barefoot, maimed, sick, poor, uneducated, brilliant, unable to march, afraid to shoot a gun, people of all ages and backgrounds. Judas was right when he saw Jesus as a man of power, but he mistook the power of the Cross for military might.

For some, Christ's saving power is yet to come and they await the end of the world. In both Nazareth and Bethlehem there is massive construction of hotels and roads and parking ramps all over because of the crowds expected in the year 2000—people who will believe the Christ will return in that year. This kind of divine intervention would mark the end of human free will as God, finally, in the twinkling of an eye, will perfect the world according to his will.

To Amos and some of the later old Testament prophets, the Messiah would bring an ethical revolution. The Messiah would herald the day when the eyes and hearts of the people would be opened; a day when we would choose to be God's people. A day when the love of our Lord would turn people's hearts around and we would treat one another fairly and follow the golden Rule; a day when the poor would share their original inheritance, a day when all debt would be forgiven, prisoners set free, slaves freed, and widows comforted. It is that Messiah of which Isaiah spoke:

"A shoot shall come forth from the stump of Jesse, and a branch shall grow out of his roots. The spirit of the Lord shall rest upon him…and the wolf shall live with the lamb, and the leopard shall lie down with the kid, the calf and the lion and the fatling together and a little child shall lead them. They will not hurt or destroy on all my holy mountain; for the earth will be full of the knowledge of the Lord as the waters cover the sea"

Who is the one crying in the wilderness, and who will prepare the way of the Lord?

Perhaps I should be asking what is the wilderness? And why do I assume it is a bad place? Perhaps my own discomfort with my own wilderness has blinded me to the biblical history of God calling a people into the wilderness. Perhaps it is our wilderness experiences that open our eyes, hearts and minds to God's will and promise. Perhaps this Christmas, instead of trying to create a lovely light-filled, present-filled oasis of perfect love, harmony, and unawareness, we should open our ears to the ones crying in the wilderness. We will discover that it is us that God is calling—Prepare ye the way of the Lord.

Preparation begins with a willingness to see the world as it is, with a willingness to change. Action is made possible by the strength and power and hope of the Holy Spirit and by the promise that God is a God of mercy and righteousness who will not leave us a dispirited, homeless, scattered people. This Advent John calls us from our comfort and plenty. John again reminds us that this time and in this place we are the voice, the hands, the word of hope and forgiveness. We must take seriously the preparing of our own hearts, our own churches, our own organizations, our own communities, for the word and the hope of salvation to be heard. If we write on the door posts of our churches: WELCOME, ALL WHO ARE BEATEN, DEPRESSED, DISCOURAGED, DEFEATED. THE GOD OF HOPE AWAITS YOU HERE, let us be prepared to make it come true.

Pam age 2

Pam and Bill Fulton

Pam age 18

A Messy affair

Acts 2:1-21

May 30, 2004

Some of you may know that the Suttons Bay Elementary School sponsors a Youth Friends program. The program links youngsters who need extra attention with volunteers who come to visit the child during school hours one or more times a week. My youth friend is a little girl in kindergarten who comes from a difficult home situation. I've only been doing this for a couple of months but I'm already pretty attached to this little kid.

Last week, my little friend wanted to paint so we got the paints out of the supply closet which is provided for us. We opened it up and my little one announced she was going to paint her hand. My instant instinct was to say "No, that's too messy." But I quelled my instinct and she painted her hand bright red, made a hand print on the paper, spilled a little paint here and there and then said she wanted to paint my hand. My instinct got the better of me and I said "No, that's too messy"—and then at her crestfallen expression I thought better of it and said "Why don't you paint a flower on my hand?" So she did. A blue and yellow one on the palm of my hand. When my little friend went back to her class I headed to the sink to wash off my flower because I knew the paint would get all over everything. Then I thought better of it. And I'm glad I did. Because I saw her three times as she was getting ready to leave school and get on the bus. Each time I saw her I pointed to my flower and was rewarded with the biggest smiles I'd seen on her face yet.

Sometimes, doing God's work is messy. I could tell you about the time Ed and I had to walk through ankle deep dead cockroaches to keep a mother from losing her children, but I'll spare you those details. The point is: doing God's work is sometimes messy.

I'm sure that all of you proud parents of graduating seniors can remember some messy times in the process of raising them up to the neat and tidy people they are now. Well, at least they're neat and tidy today.

There are other kinds of messiness as well as the obvious dirt and slime kind. There is emotional messiness. We refer to messy situations and messy divorces. I remember the time my first child, my golden child, who never did anything wrong, was brought home in the 9th grade by one of her teachers, rip-roaring drunk. You better believe things were pretty messy around our house for a while after that. Sometimes churches get in messy situations too, with conflict among members or disagreements with a minister.

And then there's spiritual messiness. And the best example I know of spiritual messiness is Pentecost. Imagine that day. The disciples and probably some others were gathered together to pray. A nice, quiet worship service. Even Congregationalists would be comfortable in that little room filled with people praying together. So dignified, so respectful. People doing what Jesus told them to do.

But then the wind blows. No little breezes these. Big gusts of mighty wind. Fire. Tongues of fire sitting on everyone's shoulder. What would you do if you turned to your neighbor today and there were flames dancing on her blouse or on his shirt? And people blathering about speaking in different languages all at the same time?

What would you think? So much noise. So much confusion. No wonder people thought they were drunk. No wonder the church has tucked this passage of Scripture up into our ecclesiastical attic. We mainline types—Congregationalists, Presbyterians, Methodists, Lutherans, and such, drag Acts 2 out from the church attic and dust it off once a year on Pentecost Sunday. We read it and honor it because it is Scripture. We ministers wear red stoles just one day a year. We celebrate just a little bit and call this day the birthday of the Church. But we keep it under control. Not too much confusion. Not too much messiness. Let's keep things neat and orderly.

If we're honest about it, this scripture about the coming of God's Holy Spirit onto all God's people is an embarrassment. It's so messy. So noisy. So confusing. People are being weird. In church. In church, of all places. The church where we want to keep things quiet. The church where we want to keep things the same. Especially when nothing is the same in our society and culture anymore. The Holy Spirit might just embarrass a church to death.

When something new happens it's always like that. New things happen when things seem messy and out of control. It's like that even in science.

Penicillin was discovered because Alexander Fleming had a messy habit of putting his used culture plates in a sink half full of antiseptic. When the stack of unwashed dishes got too high for the antiseptic bath all kinds of things started to grow. One day Fleming went in to clean up the mess (probably because he'd run out of clean culture plates) and discovered that the staphylococcus bacteria he'd grown in the dishes had disappeared. The green mold growing over the bacteria produced the antibiotic penicillin.

Penicillin was discovered because of one man's messiness. Plastic was discovered because Christian Schoenbein was "messing around"—as he called his experimenting—in his wife's kitchen. Even in science, new discoveries happen when things get messy and out of control.

That's what is happening in our Scripture lesson today. God is making something new happen. God's holy winds are blowing over the people of God. To those standing by and seeing what God was doing, it was noisy and confusing. For us sitting in our church pews, expecting everything to be the same, Pentecost seems pretty messy. Better to keep this embarrassing and messy Holy Spirit tucked up on our church attic most of the time—maybe all year.

But read on in Acts and see what God is doing. The holy wind blows. The flames of holy passion ignite the people of God. Ordinary people. People like you and me. All of them preaching about the mighty works of God. Peter the fisherman, who before Pentecost had the worst case of foot-in-mouth disease. Now preaching the gospel with such power that 3,000 people came into the church. James and John who used to fight over who was Jesus' favorite. Now John is working with Peter to heal a man who couldn't walk and James is doing other ministries. People no one had heard of before doing amazing things. Stephen, the first in the church to die for his faith. Philip, the first to go preach to the Samaritans whom everyone thought should be hated. And on and on.

It's an amazing thing what happened to that little group of people gathered together. Probably not as many people as there are gathered here. The holy winds of God blew in, and some very strange things happened. It was pretty messy. But the church and the world have never been the same again.

It happened then, it has happened again and again throughout church history. Whenever the church does not lock this messy and disturbing Holy sprit up in its attic, the church is changed.

It happened in the days of Zwingli, and Calvin, and Martin Luther. It was messy. It was called the Protestant Reformation. And the church was changed. It happened in the days of Tyndale, Cromwell, and Knox. It was messy. It was called the English Reformation. And the church was changed.

It's happening today in third world countries. Where the Holy Spirit of God has been let out of the attic, the winds of God are blowing. People come by the thousands to worship in Africa. In Korea there exists the largest church in the world, with hundreds of people gathered together. They can't build churches fast enough. People sit in trees in Africa and in Korea they worship in shifts. And the church is being changed.

It happened back then in that little church at Pentecost. It can happen here today. The holy wind of God will blow through God's church. It will happen when the church takes that key to the attic and turns the Holy Spirit loose. And what is that key? It is prayer. It happened back then in that little church at Pentecost. All throughout church history, men and women have gathered together to pray. Today in Korea where God's wind blows strong, people are meeting at the church building at 4:30 a.m. on their knees to pray. It might be messy, but the church will be changed. So, together on our knees, or in our prayer chairs, or wherever it is we pray, let us pray for wind and fire and change.

To Grieve our saints

Job 19:23-27, Luke 6:20-26

November 17, 2004

Today is All Saints Sunday—a day we set aside to honor and remember the saints of the church and the saints of our lives. As our call to worship says of the saints we honor "some have touched us personally, others have touched and called into question the institutions and structures of society but all have shaken our being."

How many people there are in that great cloud of witnesses who shake our being, who form and mold us. We couldn't begin to name them all. But what I'd like to do this morning is to focus on those we can name, those who are closest to us, who have gone on before.

I'm often struck by how rapidly we make people into saints after they've died. We mortals have a marvelous capacity for remembering only the good in people and elevating anyone we love to sainthood. My Dad died 16 years ago, and while he lived I was often angry with him for a variety of reasons—basically he committed the sin of being human. But now that he's gone I find myself tending to idolize him—to remember the good parts of our relationship and to forget the bad. I'm making him a saint. I have no explanation of why we do this, but I'm glad we do. At least it makes for happy memories rather than ones tinged with bitterness and anger. At the same time however, it makes our saints harder to part with, harder to grieve for, harder to let go.

"Blessed are those who mourn, for they will be comforted." That's Matthew's Beatitude. Luke's version of it goes like this: "Blessed are you who weep now, for you will laugh." Woe to you who laugh now, for you will mourn and weep." Mourning is a universal condition—something we all do at one time or another—probably something most of us do several times in the course of a lifetime. But for most of us, it's not a permanent condition, even though it feels that way when we're stuck in the middle of it.

So what I really want to think about with you this morning is how we grieve for our saints. A friend of mine who had recently lost someone close to her said to me with tears falling down her cheeks, "I don't know how to grieve." "It looks to me like you're doing it just fine." I said. She replied, "Oh I thought it was something you did deliberately, but if this is it then, I hate it. I just hate it."

We all hate it. Losing someone we love hurts in a way nothing else does. It's agonizing and sometimes it makes us question God's existence and all the rules by which we live. How often do we cry out when we've lost someone, "It's not fair. It's just not fair." If God exists and is truly loving and just, how could God do this to us, we want to know. There's no good answer to that question. Life is full of questions. Even Jesus spoke of questions that the wise and intelligent cannot answer—that are veiled from our understanding. But when we are grieving is when those questions come smashing and crashing into our lives. When those questions come is when we have to fall back on our faith, to hang on to our faith for dear life—the faith we've lived within for most of our lives, and eventually most of us make it through and emerge again into God's light.

There's a lot being written about grief these days. There's a lot we know about the process in psychological terms. Perhaps it's because we hear so much that we thought it was something we must do deliberately.

For a few months after my father died I found myself getting very annoyed with my professional friends who, instead of saying a simple "How are you?" would say things like "Where are you with your father's death?" I suspected they wanted an answer like, "Well, I'm done with denial and moving forward into depression but I don't understand why I've skipped the anger phase. What do you suggest?" Unfortunately, or more likely fortunately, when you're in the midst of grieving it's pretty hard to be clinical about it even if you do understand the way the process works in others. My friends were trying to be helpful and give me the opportunity to talk, which I did appreciate.

On the other hand, there still seem to be many of us who need to meet the world with a stiff upper lip, or as I would say if you were a bunch of Presbyterians, to do our grieving decently and in order. The problem is that grieving is not a decent and orderly process. Whether our grieving is done publicly or privately it involves crying and feeling yucky, and doubting and being angry, and letting ourselves feel weak and vulnerable. It means not being strong—or alternatively being strong in our weakness.

Sometimes it's not only the cultural norms that surround us that get in the way of our grieving, but our religious beliefs as well. Another friend and I were talking on the phone one day and I don't even remember whose death we were talking about but I was expressing anger or sorrow over someone's death and she said rather huffily, "Well! I'm surprised to hear a minister talk that way." Somewhat stunned I said "What do you mean?" She replied, "I always believed that when someone dies, a Christian should be happy because that person is now in God's care. To feel bad is just to be selfish."

We talked for a long time, but the essence of what I said is that God sets before us life and death and tells us to choose life. If we're to choose life then we must live it fully and we must embrace it and love it with all our being, so of course we will be angry or hurt when confronted with death, be it our own or that of one we love. We could go through life, and some do, afraid to love for fear of losing it, then we needn't experience the depths that life plunges us into, but we'd miss so much. In calling us to love, Jesus invites us to suffer. Over the course of a lifetime, you can't have one without the other. No pain, no gain—as the saying goes. Jesus wept when his friend Lazarus died and so we must weep when our friends, our parents, our spouses and lovers, our children and our saints die and leave us alone.

Nicholas Wolterstorff, author of *Lament for a Son*, whose 25-year-old son Eric was killed in a mountain climbing accident wrote, "Our culture says that men must be strong and that the strength of a man in sorrow is to be seen in a tearless face. Tears are for women. Tears are a sign of weakness and women are permitted to be weak. Of course it's better if they too are strong." "And why is it so important to be strong?" Wolterstorff continues. "I have been graced with strength to endure. But I have been assaulted, and in the assault wounded. Am I to pretend otherwise? Wounds are ugly, I know. They repel. But must they always be (covered)?"

"I shall look at the world through tears. Perhaps I shall see things that dry-eyed I could not see." Nick Wolterstoff is a courageous man in his determination to experience the fullness of his grief. The world would be a better place if we could all look at it through tears, for then we would understand the pain of our brothers and sisters who travel this life with us. And if we understood, we might do something about the pain we can prevent.

A woman in my church in Lansing related a wonderful story to me about her granddaughter and her unfinished business with her grandfather who had just died. The night before the funeral the family was gathered at the funeral home. One of the old gent's granddaughters, Melissa, was sobbing uncontrollably and the other children gathered round to comfort her. They began sharing reminiscences much as a bunch of old folks might do.

"Grandpa gave me $10 worth of pennies," said Melissa.

The others allowed as how they'd also been the recipients of such beneficence.

"Grandpa gave me his California raisin sweatshirt," said Melissa.

"He did?" queried 6-year-old Chelsea.

"Uh-hunh"

"Do you wear it lots?"

"Uh-hunh."

"Do you sleep in it?"

"Sometimes." Said Melissa.

Chelsea stood and left the group and walked over to Grandpa in his casket, looked at him and said "Grandpa, why didn't you give me that California Raisin sweatshirt?"

It's hard to let go when there are unresolved matters between you. Would that we could all deal with them as forthrightly as Chelsea did. She may not get an answer right away, but she'll probably figure it out sometime, and in the meantime she knows what the trouble is. Many of us grown-ups feel guilty about asking such questions, or weightier questions like "Why didn't you love me the way I wanted you to?" or "Why did you die and leave me alone?" So we squash the questions and feelings they evoke and our grieving processes get stuck. When grief gets stuck, joy doesn't return. We go through life being eaten from the inside out by doubts and bitterness and anger, unable to feel and embrace life.

The hardest times in grief come when we wonder if God is in control, when try as we might we cannot find God. Nick Wolterstorff reached such a point when he prayed to God these words: "Noon has darkened. As fast as she could say, "He's dead," the light dimmed. And where are you in the darkness? I learned Spy-you in the light. Here in the darkness I cannot find you. If I had never looked for you, or looked but never found, I would not feel this pain of your absence."

To have faith in the darkness is to acknowledge the darkness, to live in it, to experience it, to feel our way around in the darkness and to be willing to wait in the darkness for light to return. Would that we could always experience God's presence like a warm fuzzy blanket wrapped around us to protect us from life's storms, but it doesn't work that way. Part of suffering is experiencing God's absence and it seems that suffering is a necessary part of life. It's the part that tests us and challenges us. It's the part that makes us sensitive to the needs of others and the part that makes us grow. "In the valley of suffering, despair and bitterness are brewed," says Wolterstorff, "But there also character is made. The valley of suffering is soul making."

But you may ask, as many do, "When will grief end?" My friends, grief never ends. Grief simply changes. It finds a place to live in your heart. It is there that you get used to carrying it, it changes shape and form. Grief moves from anger and rage and bitterness and despair and comes to focus on the value of the one you loved. This change won't come in a moment or in a day. As this new grief finds its place in our hearts and makes its home there, quiet tears will still come when we least expect them. Those tears will come from the place where our grief over their death lives in the heart. With those tears we learn that a death is the end of a chapter, but it's not the end of a story. As one chapter ends, another begins, but not without the history, the presence, the love, joy, and dedication of all those who have gone before us. The story of our lives is built with a place where we carry our grief into our future.

Frederick Buechner wrote:

> When you remember me, it means that you have carried something of who I am with you, that I have left some mark of who I am on who you are. It means that you summon me back to your mind even though countless years and miles stand between us. It means that if we meet again you will know me. It means that even after I die, you can still see my face and hear my voice and speak to me in your heart. For as long as you remember me, I am never entirely lost.

Blessed are those who mourn, for they shall be comforted.

Ruth, Bob, Pam, and Bill Fulton at Ruth and Bob's 50th wedding anniversary December 22, 1984

An Invitation

Matthew 22:1-14

October 9, 2005

One day a pastor was invited to attend the children's Sunday school class. They had asked him to come to talk about what marriage means. And so the minister said: "Before I begin to talk to you, can anyone tell me what Jesus had to say about marriage?" But no one said anything, and it was very quiet. Finally, one little boy raised his hand and said: "Is that when Jesus said: Father, forgive them; for they know not what they do"?

The parable that we listened to this morning from the Gospel of Matthew deals with a wedding. Or more specifically, it deals with a wedding reception. The story starts with a king who had a son who was getting married. And so the king decided to throw a huge party to celebrate that event. And the king made out an enormous guest list, inviting as many people as he knew, inviting them to come and rejoice with him.

Now in this parable, it's not too hard to figure out who the king is supposed to be. As you probably figured out, the king represents God. And so the first thing this parable has to say to us is that our God is a God who likes a good party. Our God is a God who wants all kinds of people to come and celebrate with him.

That may not be the way you usually think about God. Most of us probably think about God as a loving God, and most often we think about this loving God in the context of bringing comfort and courage and hope in the midst of trouble. We think of God weeping because of the state of the world with its wars and environmental degradation and violence and greed. Some of us are afraid of God. I think my mother lived longer than she should have because she was so imbued with a fearful God and her sense of unworthiness. We might think of the joy of God over the birth of a baby, a young couple saying their marriage vows, the end of a war, a starving people fed. But parties? That's hardly the way we think of God. Yet we know Jesus went to parties and enjoyed being with his friends, why shouldn't God?

And when God sends out invitations, nothing makes God happier than our acceptance. When I am doing weddings often the bride or groom will ask me to check and see how filled the sanctuary is. Nothing makes them happier than for me to say "It's filled."

So in our parable, we can understand why the king became so angry. He had sent out the invitations. He really wanted those people to come. But instead, they came up with every excuse in the book.

Some people are hard to figure out. If you don't send them an invitation, they say: "How dare they do that? I can't believe they didn't invite me to their party." But if those same people had gotten an invitation, they would have said: "I can't believe they sent me an invitation. Do they really think I would attend one of their parties?"

In Miami a few years ago the city council decided that there should be a beautification committee to spruce up the town. And they figured that having 25 people on that committee would be sufficient for what needed to be done. But then the city was deluged with calls from people, all saying how they felt they should be included on that committee. So in the end, the committee had 131 members. But when the time came for the committee's first meeting, only 19 people actually showed up.

A lot of people like to be invited. They like to be on the list. But not everyone is willing to follow through. Because whenever we receive an invitation, something is always expected of us in return.

For instance, when you are invited to a wedding, it is expected that you will show up in appropriate attire. Do you groan when you receive an invitation that is black tie? I for one am very glad those invitations are far more infrequent than they used to be. I am married to a man who would have to be knocked out and hog-tied to get him into a tuxedo. But there are times when he is expected to wear a jacket and tie, and he does, although not without protest.

And back in Jesus' time, people were also expected to dress in a certain way for weddings. They didn't have tuxedos. But there was a particular kind of white robe that people were supposed to wear. And in the parable, it seems that when the time had come for the wedding reception to begin, the king walked in and looked around. But as he looked around, all of a sudden, he noticed a man sitting there, who wasn't wearing the right kind of clothes for a wedding. And so the king marched right up to that fellow and said: "Hey, buddy, what are you doing here dressed like that?" And right away the king called for his bouncers and had the man tossed out on the street and the door slammed behind him.

Now some people might be thinking to themselves, "wasn't the king unfair?" After all, what if that fellow couldn't afford to own a wedding robe? And what's more, the man was given almost no notice ahead of time. He was one of those who were invited after the first group didn't show up. Maybe his wedding robe was at the cleaners.

But back then they realized that not everyone did own a wedding robe. And so the host of a party like that would take on the responsibility of providing wedding robes for everyone who was invited. As the guests arrived, someone would meet them at the door and give them a special white robe that could slip right over what they were wearing.

And so apparently what happened here, is that this fellow just decided that he wasn't going to put a wedding robe on. We aren't told exactly why. For whatever reason, that particular man wanted the party to be a "come as you are party." But that's not the kind of party that the king had planned.

You see, several times in the New Testament, the reference is made to putting on new clothes. And what that refers to is this. Back around the time of Jesus, when people were baptized in a river, when they came out of the water, they were given a new, white robe to put on. And putting on those new clothes was a reminder of the new way of life that is involved in being a Christian.

And that's the same idea in this parable. God invites everyone to come and be a part of his kingdom. Everyone gets an invitation. But when we accept that invitation, something is expected of us. We are expected to put on that wedding robe. We are expected to put on a new way of life.

Jesus is quite clear with us. If we want to be a part of God's kingdom, then there needs to be some real changes in how we live. In the Gospel of Matthew, Jesus began his ministry by telling people to repent, to change the direction of their lives. And it was Jesus who said: "Enter through the narrow gate; for the gate is wide and the road is easy that leads to destruction, and there are many who take it. For the gate is narrow and the road is hard that leads to life, and there are few who find it."

God invites everyone to be a part of his kingdom. But that invitation is not to a "Come as you are party." Instead, it is an invitation to a "Come as God wants you to be party." "As God's chosen ones, holy and beloved" scripture tells us, "clothe yourselves with compassion, kindness, humility, meekness and patience." "Put on the whole armor of God" scripture tells us, "so that you may be able to stand against the wiles of the devil."

You know all those commercials for the armed service? Those commercials are an invitation to anyone and everyone to join the army. But for those who choose to accept that invitation, something is expected of them in return.

Because what happens when someone joins the army? In very specific ways, army recruits are taught how they are expected to live, they're told how they are expected to look in uniform, and how to make their bunk. They are made to get up at 5 a.m. and go on 5-mile runs. They are taught to look out for one another. And they are taught to see what was wrong with their old way of life, so that they can appreciate what they have by being a part of the army.

When you join the army, the drill instructor doesn't tell you to be who you want to be. If you don't want to get up at 5 a.m., you don't have the option to sleep in. You get up at 5 because that is what soldiers do. And so the job of the drill instructor is to take the recruits and turn them from what they were into what they ought to be. Because just showing up at an army base is not going to make anyone a soldier.

And it's the same with following Jesus. Just showing up at church is not going to make anyone a Christian. Instead, we become Christians as we learn how to live as Christians. As we learn how to put on that new clothing, that new way of life that comes with being a follower of Jesus Christ.

So this morning, in the name of Jesus Christ, I invite you to come to the party. For you are indeed invited. But do note that this is not a "come as you are party." Rather, it is a party where God invites you to change and to become all that you are meant to be.

48   *Wisdom and politics*

Pam Fulton on her wedding day to A. Arendt Hopeman III 1959

The Gospel is political

1 John 3:16-24, Acts 4:5-12

May 5, 2006

When I was a child I had two uncles, both of whom were journalists. Those of you who are my age or older will probably be familiar with one of them, James Reston, a.k.a. Scotty Reston, a.k.a. Uncle Scotty. Uncle Scotty was a long-time, Pulitzer-winning columnist for the New York Times. He was a Democrat. The other uncle was William Fulton, a.k.a. Uncle Bill, who, in his early years was Colonel McCormick's fair-haired boy—Colonel McCormick being the irascible, conservative Republican publisher of the Chicago Tribune. Uncle Bill's career was cut short by a severe bout of polio in his early forties. At the age of three I was proud to repeat to any who would listen "The New York Times: all the news that's fit to print" and "The Chicago Tribune: the greatest newspaper in the world."

When these two uncles got together at our house the sparks flew. They weren't just sparks, they were fireworks. My Dad was a Republican and both he and Uncle Bill ganged up on Uncle Scotty—but Scotty was pretty well able to hold his own. The wives joined in the melee too. Both my aunts were writers as well. After I'd been put to bed I would sneak downstairs and sit on the bottom step to listen. It was wonderful—all that talk of distant lands and important people and visits to the White House and governor's mansions, and the jokes that flew back and forth and the huge, explosive arguments. But they never stopped loving each other. The next morning they were just as friendly and loving as ever. They never lost respect for each other or thought the other one was a bad person or stupid.

On Sunday mornings my Dad would read Scotty's column and pace the floor, shaking his head, saying "I just don't see how he can think that way." But he never stopped loving him or respecting him or wanting to be with him.

A bad thing is happening in our country. I read a news report a couple months ago that talked about how we are more and more living and associating only with people of our own kind—people who share the same values and the same political persuasion.

It used to be said that you couldn't talk about politics, sex, or religion, but these days it is a whole lot easier to talk about sex and religion than it is to talk about politics, at least to someone who has opposing views. I think it's a shame that we can't talk politics with each other and it's one of the big factors in the increasing polarization in this country. We seem to think that if people disagree with us politically they are somehow bad people who we cannot respect and certainly, people with who we cannot be friends.

Now what's the implication of this for our church? St. Andrews is a church that prides itself on its diversity. Well, we certainly are not diverse racially, and not very diverse economically, and not very diverse in life-style. We are diverse in that we come from many religious backgrounds and we seem to be able to talk about that just fine. We are diverse politically. My guess is that we're split just about half and half, Republicans versus Democrats. And my how we clam up on that subject! We're afraid of starting an argument. We're afraid of being rejected. We're afraid of getting angry ourselves. And maybe we're afraid of having our beliefs challenged.

But, my friends, what does that do to our life together. It's like living with the proverbial elephant in the room. Everyone knows it's there but we can't speak of it. And if we cannot speak with each other about our deepest values and beliefs, how can we know each other? And if we cannot truly know each other, how can we love each other? And if we cannot love each other, how can we have the community of faith we want?

Our reading from 1 John tells us "…let us love, not in word or speech, but in truth and action… This is his commandment, that we should believe in his name and love one another just as he has commanded us." My friends, the bottom line is that if we are Christians, we must love one another—and how can we love one another if we cannot talk about what we hold dear.

Now some of you will surely say "But we can't talk about politics in church because we have separation of church and state." Well first of all, we don't really have separation of church and state. If we do, why am I, a clergyperson, allowed to legally perform marriages and why am I allowed to deduct all my household expenses from my income taxes because I am a minister?

Be that as it may, our constitution established the separation so that the government could not establish a state religion and so that the government could not interfere with religion. It was never intended to mean that churches could not talk about politics within their own bounds. It most certainly does not mean that we can or must separate our political thoughts from our spiritual thoughts. Federal tax law says that we cannot spend more than 10% of our income on lobbying or trying to influence government policies. But it doesn't say we can't talk about them. When you get in to the area of endorsing particular candidates I'm not sure how the law reads, but I've been in Catholic churches and black churches where I've seen candidates introduced and the priest or minister has urged the congregation to vote for them. I am not, however, suggesting we do that.

As an exploratory venture to see if we can talk about a political subject and still maintain our respect and friendships with one another, on May 28 the Adult Education will be a Presbyterian Church-produced discussion on Immigration policy.

All right, that's the first part of this sermon. I will go to the Bible for our second part, specifically to our lesson from Acts.

Peter and John have just spent the night in jail. They had been arrested the day before in an act of civil disobedience when they had healed a man contrary to the rules laid down by the Roman Empire's occupying force. They had done this act of healing for someone crippled from birth, someone whom everyone knew because they had seen him there every day, begging. The apostles had acted at the hour of the afternoon prayer service and this had caused a commotion. They then announced that they had done this in the name of a recently executed subversive, Jesus of Nazareth, whom they claimed was back from the grave and had resumed his subversive activity. So why were they arrested? Let me give you some background.

In 63 B.C. Rome conquered Judea, the Jewish homeland with it's capital at Jerusalem and deposed the Jewish monarchy. Traditionally Rome ruled through local collaborators whenever it could. The qualification for ruling on Rome's behalf was wealth. These collaborators were given a relatively free hand as long as their loyalty was unquestioned and they kept the local populace quiet.

In 6 B.C., when Herod the Great died, Rome placed its collaborators at the center of the temple. The temple had always been religiously important. It now became the central economic and political institution of the country. And it was the center of collaboration with Rome. It had the defining features of ancient domination systems: rule by a few, economic exploitation, and religious legitimation. The religious leaders of the temple were also collaborators with the Roman Empire. So when we hear about the "Jews" opposing Jesus, we must realize that these people were primarily responsible to the Roman Empire.

Enter Jesus. Jesus came proclaiming the "Kingdom of God"—an alternate kingdom. To first century listeners, Kingdom of God was both a religious and a political term: the Kingdom of GOD, and the KINGDOM of God. And he proclaimed that the Kingdom of God was near.

In Mark's gospel, which we've been following for this lectionary year "to believe in the good news" did not mean to believe in a set of propositions as modern-day Christians tend to mean, but to "trust in the news that the Kingdom of God is near and to commit to that kingdom"—as opposed to the kingdom dominated by the Roman Empire. Can you see why the authorities, these local collaborators responsible for keeping things quiet, were afraid of Jesus? By the time Philip and John were arrested, Luke tells us that 5,000 people were counted as followers of Jesus.

Jesus' message was preached almost exclusively to the peasants. During the time of Herod the Great, the one who died in 6 B.C., the peasants had lost ground, both literally and figuratively. Up until Herod, they had managed to subsist on their land. Under Herod, much of their land had been taken away and they had no other means of survival. The peasants lived in the rural areas in which Jesus preached. The wealthy lived in the cities. Jesus never went to a big city until he went to Jerusalem, knowing he would be killed there. The peasants were following him and pledging allegiance to this alternative kingdom. Jesus was a political figure. And Jesus had an agenda—to switch to Luke for a moment, to bring good news to the poor, to proclaim release to the captives and recovery of sight to the blind, to let the oppressed go free, to proclaim the year of the Lord's favor. That was Jesus' agenda and it was political. And if we are followers of Christ, that must be our agenda too. And it is still a political agenda.

Our problem is that pushing the agenda of Jesus clashes with our own agendas—our own wants and needs for security, wealth and power. And so we've spiritualized Jesus. We prefer a "milquetoast" Jesus who is, frankly, something of a wimp. We much prefer the Beatitudes, or as Robert Shuler says, the *Be (Happy) Attitudes*, to that of Jesus throwing the money-changers out of the temple. Jesus welcoming the little children is a preferred image to that of Jesus saying "I come not to bring peace, but a sword." If you read through the Gospels and count, you will find that there are many more challenging statements than there are words that comfort.

We sang the 23rd Psalm this morning, that most comforting of all Psalms—we think. The gospel lesson I did not use this morning is the one from John that starts out "I am the good shepherd." We love that passage don't we? Listen to what noted Old Testament scholar Walter Brueggemann says about that image:"

> The term "Shepherd" is political in the Bible. It means king, sovereign, lord, authority, the one who directs, to whom I am answerable, whom I trust and serve. In this simple opening line, the psalm is clear about the goal and focus, the center and purpose of life: (God) and not other. There is no rival loyalty, no competing claim—not economic or political, not liberal or conservative, not sexist or racist, nor any other of the petty loyalties that seduce us. It is a mark of discernment and maturity to strip life down to one compelling loyalty, to be freed of all the others that turn out to be idolatrous.

The gospel is political. Jesus was political. We are political. To say we must keep politics out of the church is an escape from the real Jesus and the real gospel. It lets us off the hook. Let's not do it anymore. We don't need to talk partisan politics. We don't need to attack each other's favorite candidates, but I do believe we can, should and must talk about political issues. And if our faith is to have any relevance for our lives in the world today we can do it with love and friendship and respect.

1. Marcus Borg & John Dominic Crossan, *The Last Week*. (Harper San Francisco), 2006 p. 2.
2. *Ibid*, pp. 7-8.
3. *Ibid*, p. 25.
4. Walter Brueggemann, *The Threat of Life: Sermons on Pain, Power, and Weakness*. Ed. Charles L Campbell (Minneapolis: Fortress Press, 1996) pp. 91-19.

Those people

John 4:5-20

September 10, 2006

If those people would only get off their duffs and do something they wouldn't be poor.

Those people are all alcoholics and druggies.

Those people are all slobs. Have you ever been in any of their houses?

You've got to be careful. You can't take chances with those people around.

Have you seen the way those people jerk their kids around? They don't care two cents for them.

Those people are getting what they deserve. After all, God helps those who help themselves.

Those people smell.

Those people probably have AIDS.

Those people make me afraid.

Those people really don't want to be with us anymore than we want to be with them.

Suppose a wild-eyed man—all tattered and torn, dirty and sick looking, smelling of alcohol walked in here on a Sunday morning to worship with us. What would be our response to him? What if he came to our coffee hour and started gobbling up all the cookies at an alarming rate. What if he went to use the bathroom to wash himself?

What would our response be?

There's Jesus talking with a Samaritan—a Samaritan woman yet—out in broad daylight! Do you know how many different men she's been with? She's working on her sixth. Jesus has no business talking or doing whatever he's doing with any woman, let alone a woman like that! Good Jews don't have anything to do with those people.

And Jesus' response to this woman was to love her and to reveal to her that he is the Messiah and send her to spread the Good News to the other Samaritans. She was the very first apostle.

What is our response to her?

Jesus, what are you doing going into that cemetery? There's a crazy guy in there. He'll kill you for sure. He's violent. They can't even keep him locked up anymore. There's no help for those people. You've got to think of yourself. Think of all the good you can do if you don't get yourself killed. It's too risky. Don't go.

And Jesus' response was to go and to love him and heal him.

What is our response to him?

Jesus, what are you doing, letting that woman rub your feet—with her hair yet. Don't you know who she is? Don't you know how she got the money to buy that ointment? She's one of those women. She's a prostitute. She might have all kinds of diseases and she certainly doesn't deserve anything from you. You're too good to have anything to do with her. Besides you're embarrassing Simon, your host. Can't you see how uncomfortable you're making him? And you certainly don't want to offend Simon. He's in a position to do you a lot of good.

And Jesus' response to her was to love her and to forgive her sins.

What is our response to her?

There is usually some truth in the stereotypes we lay on people. There are lots of mentally ill people wandering the streets of our cities and there are lots of people who are violent in our society. They can be scary—and yes, I've been scared too. There are lots of people who don't know how to keep a house or raise children and, God knows, there's a frightening epidemic of substance abusers. But we do a great disservice to "those people" and to ourselves when we are quick to apply stereotypes to whole groups of people and to label and condemn. "Judge not, and you will not be judged," says Jesus. "condemn not and you will not be condemned," says Jesus. "Forgive and you will be forgiven," says Jesus.

When we label and condemn we not only curry God's displeasure but we lose out on the chance to know the real people who live behind the stereotypes. We lose the opportunity to recognize others as our sisters and brothers in Christ—perhaps even the opportunity to meet Christ himself. And we lose the opportunity to love others and in loving, to receive love in return.

Let me tell you a story to show you what I mean. Most of you probably know by now that when I was in Lansing from the mid- 80's to the mid- 90's I was the director of Advent House Ministries. One of the things we did there was to run a weekend day shelter because homeless folks had nowhere to go during the weekend days. Lots of other folks from all over the city came too because we served breakfast, lunch and dinner, all free.

Before Ed and I were married, I guess it must have been while we were dating, Ed agreed to take over the role of volunteer coordinator for the shelter. Somewhere on one of the lists of volunteers he found the name of Jerry Morris and his phone number, so he called and signed him up to come and work at Advent House the following Saturday.

Well, I knew Jerry Morris. He was one of our regular Advent House guests, a large older man, slow-moving and slow-witted. I knew him to be an alcoholic. When Ed told me who he'd signed up to work I laughed and said "I bet you he'll never show up. He's just an old drunk, and even if he does come he won't be any good." (Now if you think I don't fall into the labeling trap, think again.)

Somehow Ed believed in this man, and he believed he'd come, or maybe he just didn't want me to prove him wrong. Jerry didn't come, of course, and I couldn't resist saying in my self-righteousness, "I told you so."

But Jerry did show up in the middle of the next week, and Ed patiently explained that it was on Saturdays, not weekdays. Jerry promised to come the next Saturday.

Somewhere in the course of their conversation Ed found out that Jerry was soon to celebrate his sixtieth birthday. Ed decided to have our Advent House bakers make him a birthday cake that he'd give to him on Saturday. "I'll bet he doesn't show" I said. Sure enough he didn't. By this time, Ed was angry with him, but not willing to write him off, so he called Jerry and told him he'd missed out on having a birthday cake by not coming.

A few days later, Jerry showed up to pick up his by then stale birthday cake. He was delighted, but he left right away. I was sure that was the last we'd see of him. I was wrong.

Jerry showed up the following Saturday and he showed up every Saturday after that for the 2 or 3 years until he died. After some initial trial and error with several tasks he decided that his job was to empty the trash—which at Advent House is a big job. And heaven help anyone who tried to step on his turf by helping. Taking out the trash was Jerry's job. He did a good job and he knew he did a good job. He had acquired a place, a niche in our community and people knew who he was. He was no longer one of "those people"—he was a real person. And to the day he died he talked about the birthday cake and how no one ever did that for him before. I'd never have given him a chance because I'd stuck a label on him. I'd made him one of "those people" and hadn't seen the person inside who would respond to being treated with dignity and respect.

There's a whole host of reasons, I suspect, why we need to label and judge and condemn the others of God's children who are different from us. Let me suggest a few.

First, there is selfishness, greed and laziness and all that blatantly sinful stuff. If we recognize others as persons of equal worth then we'd probably have to wonder why we have so much and they have so little and we might be called to give up some of our money, or not buy ourselves so many toys, or worse yet, we might have to give up our time to help and look for ways of eliminating the causes of poverty and illness and violence and substance abuse. "Give to everyone who begs from you," says Jesus, "and of one who takes away your goods do not ask them again. And as you wish that people would do to you, so do to them."

Another reason we need to lay on the stereotype by way of making excuses for our inaction, is fear—plain, cold, out-and-out fear. We are afraid of anything and anyone different. The known is good, the unknown is bad. We're afraid for our physical safety and perhaps, even more, we're afraid we'll say or do something wrong and be embarrassed.

When the disciples came and found Jesus with the Samaritan woman, I suspect their dominant emotion was embarrassment. They were afraid someone would see Jesus with her and they were afraid it would hurt his image. They may also have been afraid they would have to interact with her. Fortunately, they had the good sense not to say anything. But Jesus wasn't uncomfortable or embarrassed because he saw the woman as the person she was. He saw her shame and guilt and sadness. Because he saw her as a whole person he could love her.

"Judge not, condemn not, forgive and give," says Jesus, "for the measure you give will be the measure you get back."

A final reason, although I am sure there are others, for our need to label and condemn is that to see "those people" as real persons means that we have to see their pain, and we have to feel their pain, and that puts us in touch with our own pain and that hurts. And lots of times there's not a thing in the world we can do to make someone else's pain go away, and that hurts even more. It suggests to us that our hurts might not go away. And we work terribly hard to try and cover up our pain and not to recognize it.

"Blessed are you that weep now," says Jesus. "for you shall laugh" and "woe to you that laugh now, for you shall mourn and weep."

Jesus calls us to suffer with the poor, to suffer with the mentally ill as well as the physically ill, to suffer with the criminal and the addicts, and victims of domestic abuse and of incest, with AIDS victims. Jesus calls us to suffer with him and we do it by suffering with "those people."

Michael Christiansen, an urban minister in San Francisco learned something of how we suffer with Christ when he went to spend some time with Mother Theresa in Calcutta a few years before she died. Christiansen was shocked and repulsed by the suffering he saw there. In his book, "City Streets, City People," Christiansen says, "Everywhere I turned I was confronted with extreme disease and poverty. A half million sleep on the streets; thousands of the destitute on the threshold of death can be found near the train stations and under Howrah Bridge. Live infants are sometimes thrown into trash cans, lepers are tossed into gutters, and aging parents, rejected by their children, are left to die alone." Michael was not prepared for such poverty and he wanted to flee, to freak out in the face of suffering. After mass one morning, Michael broke down and told Mother Theresa what he was experiencing.

"Did you see Jesus?" asked Mother Theresa. Michael couldn't say that he had. All he'd seen was suffering, disease and death.

"When we love the poor," Mother Theresa said, "we do not first see the poor, we first see Jesus! We are not social workers, but missionaries of Christ's love. We do it for Jesus! And when we pick a body off the street and nurture him back to health, we do it to Jesus! It is his face we see in the faces of the poorest of the poor."

Mother Theresa took Michael's hand in hers and said, "The gospel is written on your fingers." She slowly pointed to each of his five fingers and said, carefully emphasizing each word, "You-did-it-to-me."

She brought Michael's five fingers together and said, "See the five wounds of Jesus?" Michael thought about the 2 wounds in his hands, the 2 in his feet, and the one wound in his side. Putting his pointed fingers into the palm of her hand, she said softly: "This is his love for you."

"Now close your fist," she said, "this is the sacred heart of Jesus that says to us: When I was hungry, you gave me something to eat: when I was thirsty you gave me drink; I was a stranger and you took me in, naked and you clothed me: I was sick and you visited me." "And at the end of your life," she added, "your five fingers will excuse you or accuse you of doing it unto the least of these, "You-did-it-to-me!"

Called by name

Isaiah 43: 1-7

January 13, 2007

If you're as old as I am, you can remember when there was no security in airports. Friends and family accompanied us to the gate and waited there with us and then we just got on the plane. I don't remember when security concerns at airports began and when they installed the x-ray machines. It seems that was quite a long time ago. But for a long time all you had to do was put your carry-on luggage on the conveyer belt and walk on through. Now you have to take off your shoes, and jewelry, and jacket, and you can't carry over three ounces of liquid in your carry-on. On one of my continuing education trips last year I got to the airport and discovered I didn't have any ID with me. Let me tell you, that was some process. My anxiety rose and I felt like a criminal. I got on the plane after being patted down and subjected to all manner of searches, and I felt afraid.

I think most of us feel a bit afraid going through security—and if anyone around us seems at all suspicious, then the fear heightens.

Airports exemplify the climate of fear we live in all the time as we hear about terrorism, global warming, polluted and tainted food and pharmaceuticals, and the proliferation of nuclear weapons in unfriendly countries.

The old world where we felt safe and secure is gone—probably forever. We don't know what's coming next and it makes at least some of us afraid.

How many of us who think of ourselves as people of faith say to ourselves "I don't know what's going to happen and it makes me afraid?" It's one thing to trust God, to feel close to God, to feel God caring for us when life seems stable, secure, and safe. But what happens in times when the old world where we thought we were safe and secure dies, and the mountains shake in the heart of the sea, and fearful change and terror seem to be at every hand? What happens to our faith then?

Living between a dead past and a future not yet born. That was exactly the situation of the Jews in the Bible who heard this word from the prophet Isaiah. They were between a dead past and a future not yet born. Their old world had died. What happened was that the world's great superpower, Babylon, had marched on Jerusalem, their home. Babylon had crushed Jerusalem and left it in ruins. Many Jews were taken back to Babylon as prisoners of war where they "sat by the rivers of Babylon and wept." They felt like they were pawns in a game they could not control. And then, just when it was hard to believe things could get any worse, they did. A new power, Persia, arose in the East and was rattling its sabers against Babylon. Now, once again, the Jews were in harms way in the middle of a war zone. War fears swept the city. The wheels of history were about to roll over them again, and they were living in a world not expected to last, between a dead past and a future not yet born. And they were afraid.

And then comes this amazing, almost unbelievable word from the prophet:

> But now thus says the Lord,
> He who created you O Jacob,
> He who formed you O Israel:
> Do not fear, for I have redeemed you;
> I have called you by name,
> You are mine.

Christians recognize those words of course. In fact, if I had to put the gospel of Jesus Christ into one phrase, I think it might be "Do not be afraid." It is what the angels said to the shepherds when Jesus was born: "Do not be afraid." It is the first word the angel spoke on Easter morning: "Do not be afraid." It is what the risen Christ said to his disciples: "Do not be afraid. I am with you always."

But it is one thing to say it, and another thing to believe it. As a matter of fact, in this kind of world, in a time when we are living between a dead past and a future yet to be born, why shouldn't we be afraid?

Whether we should or we shouldn't, the fact is, we are afraid.

When we think about it, our fear is not just about terrorism or global warming. Those are symptoms of a deeper fear that we are all uncertain creatures set in an uncertain place. The philosopher, Pascal, expressed it well when he said:

"When I consider the short duration of my life, swallowed up in the eternity before and after, this little space which I fill and even can see, engulfed in the infinite immensity of spaces of which I am ignorant and which know me not, I am afraid…"

And that is why the prophet Isaiah can say with confidence. *Do not be afraid, says the Lord, you are precious in my sight and I love you.* Because Isaiah knew that the Lord who spoke these words is not some distant deity, some impersonal force loose in the universe, a god pulling the strings of history. God is more like a mother who listens in the night for the cries of her children. *Do not be afraid, says the Lord, I created you. I formed you, I have redeemed you. I have called you by name, You are mine.*

The God of Israel, the God whose story is told in this scripture, always calls us by name: Adam, Eve, Abraham, Sarah, Moses, Samuel, Mary. This is the God we see in the face of Jesus Christ. The God who walks along the shore and calls by name: Peter, Andrew, James, John, follow me.

This is the God who knows your name, who knows the number of hairs on your head, the God who remembers you and does not forget you, the God who, even when the winds blow and the seas roar, listens for your voice, knows your cry and says to each of us *"Do not be afraid. I know you, I have called you by name, I am coming to help you. You are mine."*

Sixteen years ago I had the great joy of baptizing my first grandchild. As she was brought to the baptismal font in her pretty yellow dress and head full of curls, she was smiling and cooing. I poured the water of baptism on her head and said the words, "Megan Paige, I baptize you in the name of the Father and of the Son and of the Holy Spirit." Have you ever noticed how important names are in baptism? In her baptism, we called her by name—Megan Paige. And we believe that God called Megan too, and that her name was joined forever to God's name, just as all who are baptized have their names called, have their names forever joined to God's name.

Now the truth of the matter is that when she was baptized, no one knew what Megan's life was going to be like. We prayed for her health and happiness, we prayed that she would grow in faith. But we also knew that, because she is a human being, she would face pain and loss. She would, like all humans, pass through the waters of life's hardships, cross the rivers of life's pains and walk through the fire of being human. And so she has.

Megan's life has not been what we hoped for her. Although Megan has a family who loves her and has all the material goods she could want, she is not happy. She is often anxious, sometimes depressed and suicidal, and doesn't do well in school even though she is very bright. None of us understand what Megan's demons are. But we do know that God knows her name, that God created her, formed her, redeemed her, and calls her by name. God will never forget her and will be with her at every turn. So, as Isaiah says to Megan and says to you and to me, too:

> When you pass through the waters I will be with you;
> And through the rivers they shall not overwhelm you;
> When you walk through the fire you shall not be burned,
> And the flame shall not consume you.

And that is why I know that some way, some how, Megan will be all right.

A Presbyterian preacher, Tom Long, tells a story of a unique meeting back in 1976, back when we were celebrating our country's bicentennial year. At that time a very creative writer came up with an intriguing idea. Our nation is 200 years old, he thought, I'll bet I can find someone who is alive today who is old enough that when they were a child, they remember meeting someone who then was old enough to have been alive at the founding of the nation, a living link to the beginning of the country. And sure enough—he found such a person. He was a Kentucky farmer named Burnham Ledfore, who was over 100 years old in 1976; and he remembered being taken by a wagon to see his great-grandmother who was then over 100 herself, and was a little girl when George Washington was installed as the first American president.

When the writer asked Burnham what he remembered, he said he remembered being taken into his great-great grandmother's house. She was feeble. She was blind. She was sitting in the corner of a dark bedroom. "We brought Burnham to see you," his father said. The old woman turned toward the sound and reached out with long boney fingers and said in an ancient cracking voice, "Bring him here." They pushed me toward her, Burnham remembered. I was afraid of her. But when I got close to her, she reached out her hands and began to stroke my face. She felt my eyes and nose, my mouth and my chin. And all at once she seemed satisfied, and she pulled me close to her and help me tight. "This boy's a Ledford," she said, "I can feel it. I know this boy, He's one of us."

In an even deeper way when we are baptized, God holds us close and says I know this one. I called this one by name. This one belongs to me. Fear not. I KNOW YOU BY NAME.

Well-known theologian Henri Nouwen once confessed that he was plagued many nights by a terrible dream. He dreamed that he was traveling in some distant city, and he ran into someone with whom he had gone to high school. In the bad dream, the person would say "Henri, Henri, haven't seen you in years. What have you done with your life?" This question always felt like a judgment. He'd done some good things in his life. But there had also been some trouble and struggles. And when the old schoolmate in his dream would say "What have you done with your life?" he wouldn't know how to answer, how to account for his life. Then one night he had another dream. He dreamed that he died and went to heaven. He was waiting outside the throne room of God, waiting to stand before the almighty God, and he shivered with fear. He just knew that God would be surrounded with fire and smoke and would speak with a deep voice saying "Henri, Henri, what have you done with your life?" But then, in the dream, when the door to God's throne room opened he could hear God speaking to him in a gentle voice saying, "Henri, it's good to see you. I hear you had a rough trip, but I'd love to see your slides."

"Fear not says the Lord, I know you. I have called you by name. You are mine."

Pam and Megan Davidson on the day Megan was baptized.

Final words

John 13:31-35

May 6, 2007

When my father's final days came after a series of heart attacks and strokes, he lay in a crib-like bed in a nursing home in Florida, curled up in a fetal position, his eyes stuck shut with gunk, weighing about 80 pounds. He no longer recognized my mother and was unable to communicate. In those days Florida law would not let us withhold tube feeding so he probably lived several months longer than he should have.

My brother, Bill, and I went to see him one last time. We approached his bed and both of us said simply "Hi Dad." And he responded—"Pam? Bill?" We told him we loved him and he responded again "I love you." This from a man who rarely said "I love you" when we were young. Have you any idea how much that couple of minutes with my Dad and his final "I love you" meant to me? He died shortly afterwards.

Final words are important. When I am with families who have just lost a loved one, they almost always tell me about the last days and hours and minutes and, if the person was at all conscious, what he or she said. How we treasure those final words from someone we love! They stay with us, usually forever.

Today's lectionary reading returns us to the final words of Jesus as told by John. Judas has left the room, Jesus has eaten with his disciples for the last time and washed their feet, and now he begins his final words to them. So little time, so many things to tell them. But the essence, the command he leaves us with, is "Love one another as I have loved you. Just as I have loved you, so you should love one another.

By this, everyone will know you are my disciples, if you have love for one another."

There is actually nothing original or brand new in these words. The commandment to love one another goes back much, much further than Jesus. It is one of the themes cited in the Old Testament over and over again. And Jesus certainly repeated these words often enough as he walked from village to village in Galilee and on his way to Jerusalem. What, then, was so special and memorable about these words that Jesus made them his final mandate to his disciples? Why did Jesus choose this?

I think it was that qualifying phrase, "As I have loved you," that Jesus added to the old words "Love one another." He made it quite specific by saying that they should love as he had loved them. In other words, the unique way that Jesus had incarnated that ancient ideal was to become the pattern of how the disciples, including us, were to love one another. How then are we to love as Jesus did?

St. Augustine offers us some help with this question. He once observed that Jesus loved each person he had ever met as if there was no one else in all the world to love. Jesus never failed to focus on the particular, on what was unique in each person he met. What an extraordinary commitment! Surely in all the people he met, in all his travels, he must have been tempted to lump people together in categories, in classes, in all kinds and sorts of people.

Hard as this example is to follow, I do not believe it is beyond the possibility of each of us. It is an ideal, an aspiration, to which we each can commit, even if we know that only Jesus could fully realize it.

I've always liked the story about the little boy who is trying to learn the Lord's Prayer, and one night as he knelt by his bed, these words came out:

"Our Father, who art in heaven. How do you know my name?"

Hard as it sounds, doing what Jesus did in loving each person as if there were no one else in all the world is at least an ideal toward which we can reach even if it always remains utterly beyond our grasp.

The second help we get from St. Augustine is the understanding that Jesus loved all people as he loved each person. The way he loved was not only individualized, it was incredibly universal. Even when the words Jesus spoke assumed a note of harshness, it was because of concern for those to whom he spoke. He never spoke words of contempt or disdain. We must never forget that the opposite of love is not hate or anger or hostility. Rather, the opposite of love is indifference. But there is not one example in all the gospels of Jesus ever turning away from another as if what happened to that one made no difference to him. Indifference, that opposite of love, is more of a problem for most of us than malice. Often, just not seeing another is deadlier than our hate or anger.

Years ago, a newspaper carried a story about a reporter who was covering the war in Sarajevo. The reporter noticed a little girl walking slowly in front of him. He was surprised to discover that she had been severely wounded by sniper fire. Before the reporter could react, a man rushed over and scooped up the little girl and pleaded with the reported to drive to the hospital. Without hesitating, they loaded her in the back seat and took off for medical help. After a minute or two, the man said urgently, "Please hurry, she is dying!" The reporter drove faster. A minute later the man said "Hurry, please, my little girl is still breathing." The reporter sped on. After another minute or two, the man said "Hurry please, my little girl is still warm." Soon they pulled up to the hospital, but it was too late. The girl had died in the man's arms.

The man and the reporter walked somberly to the restroom to wash the little girl's blood from their hands. As they were walking the man said, "Now comes the hardest part." What is that?" asked the reporter. The man said "Now I have to go and find that little girl's father and tell him she is gone." The reporter was stunned and said "But I thought you were the father. I thought she was your child." The man replied, "Aren't they all our children." Aren't they? Aren't we all God's children?"

God never intended his boundaries to be less than the whole world. None of us have a monopoly on God's love. And none of us can pick and choose who we will love. Pierre Teillard de Chardin said it best, I think, when he said "It is impossible to love Christ without loving others, and it is impossible to love others without moving nearer to Christ.

Then, there's that other sentence in these final words of Jesus: "By this everyone will know that you are my disciples, if you have love for one another." To love one another is to be the disciples of Jesus. Love links us to him, and it shows we are participating in his life and his kingdom. We can wear his name yet serve another. The litmus test of our loyalty to him is how we love one another.

Where is Christ? It is a large question in John's gospel. Where did he come from? Where is he going? Where have they put his body? Where is the church? Not in a building or a cathedral, not where Presbyterian order or correct interpretation of the Bible are honored, but "Where two or three are gathered in my name." And where is that? It is where we love one another.

There's a lot of talk around this church about how we will fare in the future. Will we be able to pay off this building? Will we keep growing? How can we get younger people? You know the questions. I submit to you that the success of failure of this church will not ride on how much money we raise or how fast we grow or what kind of people join the church. The success or failure of this church will depend on how we love each other.

Why did Jesus use these words about loving for his final commandment to us? Simply stated, it is the most important. When you have little time left, you carefully pick the words that are the most important. Jesus would not have given us this new commandment if it had not been possible for us to do. As we continue to grow in Christ we will continue to grow in love.

You and I, with the help of God's unfailing grace, can grow into the wonder of loving each one as if there is no one else in all the world to love and loving all the people in the whole world as we love each one.

Pam Fulton and Ed Havitz summer 2008